FROM BA

How Music Started

A lighthearted look at Music through the Ages

By K. R. Hillyer

*To: Rick & Sandy
Old friends are hard to find
KRR
(+ Donna)*

☹ + 🎵 = ☺

FROM BACH TO THE BEATLES
How Music Started

A Lighthearted Look at
Music Through the Ages

Copyright © 2013 by K. R. Hillyer
All rights reserved under the International and Pan-American
Copyright Conventions. Printed in the United States of America.
No part of this book may be reproduced or transmitted in any
form, by any means, without written permission from the author.

Published in the United States by
K & D Enterprises, dba
Aardvark Publishing
Seal Rock, Oregon

Manufactured in the United States of America
by Newport LAZERQUICK in conjunction with Dancing Moon Press.

ISBN: 978-1-937493-43-1

Library of Congress Control Number: 2008901095

Hillyer, K. R.
From Bach to the Beatles
How Music Started
A lighthearted look at
Music through the Ages
1. Title; 2. Northwest Author; 3. Humor; 4. Composers;
5. Music History and Biographical Snippets

First Edition
April 2013

VOLUNTARY SERVITUDE

This book is dedicated to My Love Mate,
My Chief-Cook-and-Bottle-Washer
And my Best Friend –
All of whom happen to be My Wife, Donna –
Without whom I literally could not exist.

Several of the Illustrations in this book have streamed
from the talented hands of Cortney Voss.
She is a student at Newport High School, Oregon.
I am grateful to her and – yes – she did get paid ... some.

Cover Art designed and beautifully rendered by Ed Cameron
of Newport, Oregon

Written by K. R. Hillyer[*]

---

[*] This guy is responsible for having written Way-Too-Many Bank Checks in payment of various-and-sundry Monthly Bills.

(And a couple Short Stories.)

TABLE OF CONTENTS

REQUIRED READING!

Pre-word	AUTHOR, AUTHOR!	vi
Forewarning	MAKING EXCUSES	vii

OPTIONAL...

Chapter 1	IN THE BEGINNING	p. 1
Chapter 2	HOW MUSIC STARTED	p. 2
Chapter 3	LEAPING AHEAD	p. 3
Chapter 4	ALSO BACK THEN	p. 5
Chapter 5	FROM THE "MIDDLE" MIDDLE AGES...	p. 7
Chapter 6	...THROUGH THE "LATER" MIDDLE AGES	p. 9
Chapter 7	LET THERE BE LIGHT	p. 11
Chapter 8	LET'S GO FOR BAROQUE	p. 17
Chapter 9	OTHER BROKE COMPOSERS	p. 18
Chapter 10	MORE OTHER BROKE COMPOSERS	p. 24
Chapter 11	THERE WILL ALWAYS BE CHANGE	p. 27
Chapter 12	CLASSICAL (Part One)	p. 30
Chapter 13	CLASSICAL (Part Two)	p. 34
Chapter 14	EVEN MORE CLASSICAL	p. 38
	(Please, enough!)	

Chapter 15	HERE'S WHAT'S HAPPENING NEXT…	p. 41
Chapter 16	ROMANTIC - EARLY (First Love)	p. 42
Chapter 17	ROMANTIC - MIDDLE (Net Serve)	p. 50
Chapter 18	ROMANTIC - LATE (Foot Fault)	p. 59
Chapter 19	OPERA (Not-My-Fault)	p. 70
Chapter 20	COMING ATTRACTIONS!	p. 87

ALSO FASCINATING…

Appendix A	BACH's Influence	p. 95
Appendix B	The Mass, Requiem and Stabat Mater	p. 96
Appendix C	Some Other Important Musical Forms	p. 97
Appendix D	Musical Eras	p. 100
Appendix E	MOZART's Influence	p. 101
Appendix F	Humor in Music	p. 102
Appendix G	BEETHOVEN's Influence	p. 106
Appendix H	Emotion in Music	p. 108
Appendix I	UNDER THE Influence	p. 112
Appendix J	Counterpoint and Development	p. 113

NOT-TO-BE-MISSED…

Index of Composers	p. 119
Glossary	p. 126

AUTHOR, AUTHOR!

K. R. Hillyer was not UNDER THE INFLUENCE (see Appendix I) when he wrote this book. The idea was brewing, like a good German lager, for years.

K.R. has been, at times, a businessman, a Jack-of-some-trades and a Teacher. Since he holds a B.A. in Music Education, he may actually KNOW some Music stuff.

Humor has engorged his life, much as a large ego dots his "I". He is famous for his succinct reply to that timeless imponderable "Why did the Caterpillar Cross the Road?"[*]

Hillyer and his wife lived in Germany 13 years. (No, they are not FROM Germany. They just like the country and its people.) Both have traveled a lot - most excitedly in 2009 through Europe with their two teenaged grandkids.

The enormous income from this book alone will certainly facilitate their grandiose retirement at the Central Oregon Coast.

Irving Q. Schwartz
Authority of Renown

(Written just for this book at his palatial estate near Haydn-in-the-Busch, Black Forest Cherry Cake, Germany.)

---

[*] The incredibly clever answer is somewhere in this book.

__MAKING EXCUSES__

This short book is meant to ENTERTAIN. It is best never to take oneself - or anything written herein - too seriously.

Music developed all over the world. Most of what you read here tells the tale of "Western" Music.

More exotic influences, such as Oriental or African - though important in their own right - are seldom mentioned in this book, mainly because I don't know much about them.

Despite this author's tiresome efforts, some learning will undoubtedly occur. Take it for what it is worth and be grateful, as it may not happen often.[*]

If offense is taken to something said, none was meant. Music is the 2nd greatest force in my life. I respect it profoundly.

K. R. Hillyer
No particular Renown

(Written just for this book at his one-room hovel near Sunova Beach, Central Orygun Coast.)

---

[*] Footnotes are marked throughout the book. They may, at times, provide actual enlightenment.

There are also Apenda ... Appenndi ... Lists of stuff just kinda hanging out back there near the rear cover. You will find, furthermore, a Glossary and an Index.

From Bach to the Beatles – How Music Started

1. IN THE BEGINNING

Bach did not invent Music. He had 20 children. Talk about distractions! How did he find the time to write all that Music?

Mrs. Bach (pronounced: Baa - #gq%ch&) must have raised the kiddies (There were actually two of her).[*]

'Cause Johann (Yo-hawn) wrote an awful lot of Music.

Most of Bach's ideas were brilliantly new. His Music has impacted composers for over 250 years!

And Music didn't die when the Beatles split up. Their break-up marked the end of an era for Rock and Roll. Music moves on.

It just sounds slick - *From Bach to the Beatles*.

I picked these two points as book-ends for a look at Music through the Ages.

This should be easy reading. If you peruse it light-heartedly, you'll see that's how it's written.

So, enjoy!

---

[*] The first "missus" died and he re-married. Only 10 of their 20 children survived into adulthood. Skip this footnote to avoid a "downer".

Bach was German. There will be others.

From Bach to the Beatles – How Music Started

2. HOW MUSIC STARTED

Sid Caesar probably got it right.

In the Mel Brooks Movie: *History of the World, Part I*[*] Caesar discovers Music in a cave by dropping stones onto the feet of his unsuspecting Compadres.

Some other pre-historic guy, Og, blew on one end of a piece of bamboo and it made a good sound.

Later, he learned that punching a couple of holes in this early flute made it sound even better.

And then another buddy of Sid and Og, Other Og, stretched a Targ skin across an un-used pot and beat on it with a couple of bones.

Two more "cave-ies", Og III and Jamie, added a tune and a 3rd part. Sid provided some grunts, and together they rocked the cave.

To their surprise, and our continued amazement today, their parents did not "dig" this new trend in sound.

But that's how Music was born.

Music is, simply: MELODY, HARMONY and RHYTHM.[†]

---

[*] Some of which is a very funny Movie.

[†] There are a few really GOOD things to remember from this book. This is one of them.

3. LEAPING AHEAD

For about a million years, nothing happened.

Well … that's not exactly true.

Babylon (Baab-ee-lawn) had Hanging Gardens which were a Wonder of the Ancient World.

Folks would just stand there and watch Fuchsias (Few-shahs), or *Myrtales Onagraceae,* which means "Pretty Flower".

(This is just me showing off by saying, "I know Latin!")

That kept the Babylonians way too busy to spend any time with Music. Their civilization is no longer around, so you can draw your own conclusions.

In Mesopotamia there were Mesopotamians (Mess …uh… I'm not even gonna try… The word is Arabic for "always at war.")

These people invented pottery (such as used in the Movie: *Ghost*).*

This glorious Ancient Civilization of Mesopotamia gave rise to the present Civilization of Iraq.

Obviously the concept of Harmony developed elsewhere.

---

* Some of which is a very SEXY Movie!

And…I really DON'T know Latin.

From Bach to the Beatles – How Music Started

Ancient Egyptians dearly loved their cats (Katz).

It's a pretty good bet that one day an ancient Egyptian accidentally stepped on a cat's tail…

So, they knew about Melody!

In Greece there was Drama – just like today, but without the pollution and chaos. Also what they called a "Chorus".

Pretty boring, really - just chants with no Melody.

The Greeks were busy discovering other things such as Democracy and the Hypotenuse.

(Don't ask.)

4. ALSO BACK THEN

In Ancient Rome, they had Lyres (Liars) and Drums.

African slaves brought the Drums. (It may not be PC, but it's true!)

Nero "fiddled" while Rome burned - a neat trick, as the Violin wasn't invented yet.

Around the year 500, Rome fell ...

...and nobody picked it up.

From Bach to the Beatles – How Music Started

The <u>Holy Roman Empire</u> came next, but it wasn't really Roman and not very holy.

It hung around for about 1,000 years. These people had no electric lights so they called it the Dark Ages.

The Church[*] had a "lock" on just about everything and everybody.

Monks (munks) had nothing to do but copy Scripture and make Wine (in the dark). They also drank a lot of the wine.

More importantly they learned how to brew Beer (and how to drink it).

The Monks (munks) sang Gregorian Chants (Gray-Gory-Ann). Perhaps one needed a bit of drink for courage to sing them.

These were named after their Pope, Gray-Gory-Ann (the First) who also hung around for about 1,000 years, I guess.

Gregorian Chants have a monotonous Melody with no Harmony and even less Rhythm.[†]

(Well, maybe an African Drum.)

Nuns did none-of-the-above. So much for gender equality.

These were, after all, the Dark Ages.

---

[*] We refer to the Catholic Church, descended from Rome. It was the one continuous power from the Dark Ages into the Renaissance.

[†] Gregorian Chants are slow; nothing and nobody moves. To truly have rhythm, SOMETHING has got to MOVE.

5. FROM THE "MIDDLE" MIDDLE AGES…

The World was covered with a whole lot of Individual Poor People. There were a few Rich Guys in Castles, a couple cities, but a general lack of organization.

There was the occasional King, but King-like stuff kept him busy. A Court Jester provided some Music to the King and his Rich Castle Guy friends.

(NOTE: The next part is not about actual Music. You could skip it but it DOES have some <u>blood and gore</u>!)

Common folk stayed home and just tried to live.

Frequent Rampaging Hordes of Barbarians would:

- rape and pillage their buildings,
- pillage and rape their crops,
- KILL THEM,
- set fire to their women and children,
- drink all their Beer,
- smash through their fields and streams,
- steal all their remote controls,
- and KILL THEM some more.

This made life difficult, at times.

From Bach to the Beatles – How Music Started

Wanderers, called Troubadours (True-bad-doors) or Minstrels brought relief to the ordinary folk by way of Stories, usually sung with a Guitar or Recorder.

There was also the occasional Red Cross Care Package.

Sometimes a few Musicians got together. Primitive Strings and Flutes were about all they had, except maybe a Drum (having originated, perhaps, in Africa).

And let's not forget about those Gregorian Chants.

Exciting.

Gregorian Chant (Gray-Gory-Ann)

6. ...THROUGH THE "LATER" MIDDLE AGES

We're almost up to Bach!

Early attempts at organizing Music were usually Dances, Ballads and other Stories.

New Instruments came along:

- Organ and Harpsichord (forerunners of the Piano),
- Brass (think Trumpets and Horns),
- better Winds (think Flutes),
- more Drums (think Africa).

Writers started to group the short musical pieces into bigger Musical Forms such as Masses, Concertos (Kon-chair-toes), Oratorios (Oreos), Operas, Suites (Sweets), Symphonies and Ballets (Pretty Dancers).[*]

Around 1450 in Germany, Mr. Gutenberg invented movable type - a way of printing multiple copies.

Now musical ideas could spread easily to other Kings and Rich Guys.

Sometimes even the rest of us could see and hear it.

---

[*] These larger forms developed mostly in the 1700s. That means Bach (and contemporaries) followed by Haydn (hide-n), Mozart, Beethoven and other Classicists. See Appendix C for more.

From Bach to the Beatles – How Music Started

Early Moveable-Type Printing Press.

Present-day Musical Notation.

7. LET THERE BE LIGHT

In the middle 1400s, somebody said: "Hey, guys, if we're ever going to get to the 21st Century, we'd better start changing things NOW!"

So he invented the _Renaissance_ (Runny-sauce).

The _Renascimento_ (Italian) began in Italy - the same place that gave the World: Pasta, the Fiat (so-called automobile), Mussolini, Sewers, Gucci (Goo-chee), and a new government every nine months since World War II.[*]

Whenever there is a significant historic change (and that's what the Renaissance was), there are bound to be power struggles.

Most of these difficulties centered in northern Italy, specifically around three dominions or "families".

The famous (or infamous) three were: Borgia, Sforza and Medici.

Borgias were the interlopers (from Spain) who managed to get two of their family elected Pope and marry into the Sforza family that hung around Milan (northern Italy) in those days.

---

[*] There have been roughly 90 different governments in charge of Italy since the end of World War II (1945). That's a NEW group trying to get organized about every 8.9 months. I think the longest government lasted about 27 months.

And besides, Marco Polo brought back spaghetti from CHINA in the 1200s.

From Bach to the Beatles – How Music Started

History often paints general pictures. It portrays the Borgias as conniving, debauching, cheating and murdering - but in between that, they also promoted the Arts.

The Medici family comes out looking like good guys. The artists they championed were more famous – and they got <u>four</u> Popes! Medici-sponsored artists included Painters, Sculptors, Writers and Thinkers like:

Botticelli, Raphael, Michelangelo (Mike), Machiavelli (Mack), the Uffizi Gallery and Galileo (a local wine).

You don't suppose the Medici - like the Borgias - may have "bent the rules" occasionally?

<u>A Medici Prince</u>

From Bach to the Beatles – How Music Started

It would be really easy, now, to launch into a discussion of politics in the Renaissance. I am not going to do that.

New ideas were springing from fertile minds in every field – science, Philosophy, visual arts and Music . . . These clashed (or crashed) headlong with that most powerful entity, the Medieval Church.*

Renaissance Music

Composers now felt more free to "break the bonds" of Dark Ages Music.

Instruments developed from simple lutes, recorders and organs to violins, guitars, a variety of wind instruments and other keyboards (leading to the Piano). Voices found broader ranges.

Typical Musical Forms were the "three M's" – Masses, Motets and Madrigals. (See Appendix C.)

The Church tried to stop all this radical new stuff, mainly by meeting in Trento, Italy for 25 Sessions of a Council.

But change happened anyway – especially in Music.

I will mention five Composers who were important in this era. Each man will appear only briefly.

---

* Reminder: we're talking about the Catholic Church, referred to in a footnote seven pages back.

From Bach to the Beatles – How Music Started

Palestrina

Giovanni Pierluigi da Palestrina (of Palestrina) was born in Palestrina, near Rome, Italy in 1525 or 1526. He was an organist.

His later personal life was tough. Three rounds of the Plague hit Europe in 1572, 1575 and 1580. Palestrina lost his brother, two sons and his wife to the disease.

G.P. "da" wrote 105 Masses, over three hundred Motets, about 140 Madrigals and more.

Overwhelmingly his works were religious, but some of the Madrigals had "profane texts" as they were called by the Church (meaning secular or everyday).

G.P. died in 1594.

Lassus

Belgium is part of the northern European lowlands. Orlande (or Orlandus or Roland or Orlando) di Lassus was born there in about 1530. It was not a country yet, but . . . oh well.

Lassus' musical sojourn took him to Italy, back to the low countries and eventually to Munich (or München), Bavaria which is in southern Germany today.

He was a singer of excellent voice (apparently) and wrote a SLEW (that means a whole lot!) of pieces.

From Bach to the Beatles – How Music Started

Orlando penned sixty Masses, more than 500 Motets, over 150 Madrigals and two hundred or so French and German songs.

Lassus died in 1594 (same as Palestrina), but not before he established the "Florida Connection".[*]

Byrd

The lifetime of William Byrd, born @ 1540 in England, spanned the reigns of Henry the Eighth and Elizabeth the First, as well as Shakespeare. Good timing, Bill!

Byrd wrote about 470 compositions, some religious, some not. He died in 1623.

Author John Baldwin wrote this about Byrd and his Music:

". . . An Englishman, by name, William BIRDE for his skill Which I shoulde heve sett first, for soe it was my will . . ."

Gabrieli

Meanwhile, back in *Sunny Italia*, there existed one Giovanni Gabrieli, born around 1555. He studied in München with Lassus for a while (see above).

---

[*] Orlando, Disney World, Cape Kennedy . . . See Chapter 19, Opera, Vivaldi.

From Bach to the Beatles – How Music Started

Gabrieli's Music is uncomplicated. He made good use of dynamics (loud and soft) as well as the "natural" acoustics of his churches. He often stationed singers or small groups of instruments in separate "corners" – call them early Sound Effects, if you will.

Gabrieli's couple hundred pieces include about sixty choral works and 75 Concerti (see Concerto, Appendix C).

Praetorius

Michael Schultze (Italianized into Praetorius) was a German, born @ 1571, and influenced by the Italians of that time. He wrote dozens of choral numbers and other "publications" which include Motets, Chorales and more.

The ancient tune *Es ist ein Ros' entsprungen* was famously harmonized by him. Maybe you've heard: "Lo, how a rose e'er blooming". . . ?

He totaled about 180 choral pieces, including two of special note:

Am Wasserflüssen Babylon,* and

Ach, Gott in Himmel!, which became the standard for EVERY German who ever lived to SHOUT OUT, when he hits his thumb with a hammer.

---

* "At the Waters of Babylon", a very difficult piece. We're not exactly sure how Michael managed to row that boat ashore . . .

8. LET'S GO FOR BAROQUE

J.S. Bach

Bach was born in 1685 - exactly 306 years before my granddaughter. There was already Music around and he learned it.

Bach's job was to write Music, mostly for Organ, play it (mostly Organ) and teach it (mostly Organ). For this he got paid.

Johann experimented A LOT. He tried different kinds of Music, different keys, many Instruments (mostly Organ and Voice, but also Orchestra), and different modalities.[*]

Bach's influence on Music was huge!

(Oops…I already said that in the footnote.)

Johann Sebastian set the standard for all later composers. He "tempered" Music, literally perfected the Fugue (few-g), and laid down a ton of Music in two styles, usually termed Horizontal and Vertical.

He did all this before the U.S. was even a country!

---

[*] Bach's influence on Music was huge! There's a lot of confusing stuff about this in Appendix A.

Remember I said some of this stuff could actually impart knowledge? Well, this could.

Or it might be used as a sleep aid.

9. OTHER BROKE COMPOSERS

Surprise! J.S. Bach was not the ONLY Baroque composer. Among his notable contemporaries were Purcell (Purse-L), Vivaldi, at least three Scarlattis, four Pachelbels (Tah-co-bell), Buxtehude and one George Frideric Handel.

Also, one of Bach's sons (C.P.E.) is particularly important. He will show his face very soon.

The Scarlattis

The Scarlatti family was from southern Italy and Sicily.

As far as we know, the Scarlattis were NOT connected in any way to the <u>Corleones</u> or any other infamous southern Italian Family (if you catch my innuendo).

Besides, these particular Organizations (to which I refer only obliquely and with deep respect) were not even around yet.

And - you've probably already figured this out - they were ...yes.... characters from a movie.

Allesandro (father) Scarlatti was born in 1660 and is known for his vocal Music and for producing musical sons (although J.S. Bach was more active in the latter arena).

From Bach to the Beatles – How Music Started

Papa Scarlatti wrote a Stabat Mater and over 50 Operas along with Cantatas and Masses.[*]

One Scarlatti son - who had two names, Pietro (Pete) and Filippo (Phil) - wrote a lot of Keyboard pieces and an Opera.

He was the eldest and therefore died first (1750).

Vivaldi

Antonio Vivaldi, (Tony), was Italian, born in 1678, but was ALSO not associated with the Corleo…

(Uh…let's not go there again.)

Vivaldi wrote a Stabat Mater and a ton of Operas, Oratorios (Oreos) and Concertos (Kon-chair-toes). If I counted correctly, there are more than 600 of these major works![†]

---

[*] There's a brief outline of the Mass in Appendix B. For Opera, see Chapter 19. For Stabat Mater, also refer to Appendix B.

Do you ever wish you were a Medici? A Borgia? Shame on you!

[†] These Musical Forms are listed in Appendix C and sometimes B. And yes, Opera is still covered in Chapter 19.

Have you ever noticed the "De-civilizations" history presents us? Look at Pharaoh's Egypt and Egypt today. How about Mesopotamia versus Iraq? Ancient Greece compared to Greece now? Or Ancient Rome and present-day Italy? Compare also Early America to Cleveland…

From Bach to the Beatles – How Music Started

One set of 4 Vivaldi Violin Concertos is famous. It's the so-called Four Seasons or *Le Quattro Stagnioni*.

(Here I am showing off my limited knowledge of Italian.)

And, yes, they are titled "Spring", "Autumn", "Winter" and "Summer", in that weird order.

Purcell

Henry Purcell (b. approx. 1659) wrote about a thousand musical pieces, some religious, some not-so. Also, one Opera and 5 or 6 "Semi-Operas" (whatever THOSE are).

Purcell was English. He died early, when he was about 35 or 36. Mozart died at thirty-five, but Purcell was ahead of him.[*]

---

[*]In 2009, Pete Townsend of the 1960's Rock group The Who acknowledged Purcell's influence on the Rock Opera *Pinball Wizard* and other Songs.

Are Fuchsias (Few-shahs) anything like Pansies?

See Appendix F for hilarious musical hi-jinks

From Bach to the Beatles – How Music Started

BULLETIN

There follows an IMPORTANT LEGAL NOTICE. Please read it. My lawyers thank you.

- ➢ Start of IMPORTANT LEGAL NOTICE.

There is no LEGAL PROOF that any of these recently-mentioned deaths could possibly be tied to organizations with names like Our House (Mah-fee-ya) or the I - - - - Republican Army or the Elks Club or the Girl Scouts or such.

- ➢ End of IMPORTANT LEGAL NOTICE.

Pachelbel (Tah-co-bell)

Johann Pachelbel was a German Organist best known for his Organ Chorale Preludes and Fugues (few-gz).

He and the Missus had seven kids. At least three of his sons were pretty good musicians, too. There were J.M. and W.H., also Organists and C.T. (crazy Charlie), who moved to America in 1734.

We think Papa Pachelbel met Bach at a wedding when J.S. was nine.[*]

---

[*]Father Pachelbel (Tah-co-bell) died in 1706, when Bach was twenty-one. J.S. Bach lived until 1750. Pachelbel's three musical sons died in 1750 (C.T.), 1764 (W.H.) and (J.M.) who I guess did NOT die.

From Bach to the Beatles – How Music Started

Buxtehude

- Dieterich, Diderich or Diderik Buxtehude was born:
- in 1637, 1638 or 1639,
- in Germany, Denmark or Sweden.

Back then, the countries changed a lot but people pretty much stayed the same.

"Buck" (pronounced Bucks-ta-hoo-da) was a great Organist. His Organ writings were a big influence on J.S. Bach.

Bach WALKED (!) all the way to Lübeck in 1705 just to hear "Buck" play. Remember, there were no paved roads.

He stayed about three months.*

---

* The Bach walk to Lübeck was around 250 MILES (!). Bach was 20 years old and Buxtehude was to die two years later, so good timing on his (Bach's) part.

Former U.S. President Calvin Coolidge died in 1933.

Have you ever played an African Drum? Think about it. It's perfect for driving family members bananas.

Do you sometimes wish YOU were a Medieval Monk (munk) and all you had to do was write and drink?

Do you ever wish you were a Medieval Nun? (Oh, please!)

From Bach to the Beatles – How Music Started

Handel

George Frideric Handel (German: Händel), was German but ended up being one of England's most famous composers.

Handel and Bach were born the same year (1685).

G.F. wrote Operas, Oratorios (Oreos), Suites (Sweets), and a whole mass (mess) of other Music.[*]

One well-known Suite is the _Water Music_ written for King George's barge party on the Thames (Temms) River.[†]

Handel's _Messiah_ is a very famous Oratorio (Oreo) about the life of Christ.

One time, at the start of the _Hallelujah Chorus_ from that Oratorio (pronounced "Messiah"), King George stood up - supposedly.

To this day EVERYBODY stands when it is played.

Copycats!

---

[*] More impressive stuff about these forms appears in Appendix C. You could look again at some of the footnotes, Appendices A and B, Wikipedia, any REAL Music book with actual knowledge in it, or Do-Not-Pass-Go, Do-Not-Collect-200-Drachmas...

[†] See Appendices C and F for more watery Music.

If this is too boring, check out Appendix F, Humor. (Could it be I might have mentioned that previously?)

10. MORE OTHER BROKE COMPOSERS

Now, before you go crying: "Look! These guys are all German or Italian", I interject here a few exceptions.

Well …OK… two of them are Italians, but, hey – Let Not Thy Vitriol Obfuscate Thy Lobotomy!*

Couperin

A prominent French musical family, the Couperins date back to the 1560s. From grandfather through grandsons, the Couperin (Coo-pear-aaanh) heritage culminated with François.

Frank (Fran-swah) - the "Great" - composed a couple hundred Songs, mostly for Harpsichord. Frank culminated in 1733.

Rameau

Another French composer, Jean-Philippe Rameau (d. 1764) was also a talented Harpsichordist. He wrote about thirty or so Operas and Ballets (see Chapter 19, ahead).

Rameau (Ram-oh!) is easy to listen to. So is Couperin.

---

* I do not, for the life of me, know what these words mean.

Corelli

There was a Dude named Arcangelo Corelli, born in 1653 in (you're right) Italy. Corelli was from the Province of "Ferrara".

There is NO official account of Corelli driving the Famous Sports Car of similar nomenclature.*

Corelli's Car?

"Angel" Corelli was a violinist who also influenced J.S. Bach.

Some of his Music is heard in the Movie: *Master and Commander: The Far Side of the World*.

(See also Boccherini, up ahead in CLASSICAL.)

---

* The Lamborghini

From Bach to the Beatles – How Music Started

Pergolesi

Giovanni Battista Pergolesi, (John "Batty" Pear-go-lazy) Violinist and Organist, (ho hum, another Italian) had the misfortune to die of Tuberculosis at 26.*

"John" started writing at age 15 for a series of patrons. He managed several dozen pieces in his very short life - including at least two Operas, <u>L'Olimpiade</u> and <u>Il Flaminio</u> (1735).

It seems these two Operas involve the Olympic Games Torch Lighting Ceremony.

However, Pergolesi might not have known about that, since the Games didn't happen until the 20th Century.

News traveled SO slowly back then.

---

* Pergolesi holds the <u>Record</u> for dying young.

11. THERE WILL ALWAYS BE CHANGE

Sometime about now, folks got tired of being Baroque, so they decided to become Classical.

A few stopped off along the way and called it Rococo (Raw-cocoa). That lasted maybe 20 years.[*]

C.P.E. Bach

C.P.E. Bach was one of J.S.'s sons. C.P.E. stood for "Can't Publish Ennything" (actually, Carl Philipp Emanuel). He was important in this "transition" period.

A lot of soon-to-be-famous guys like Beethoven, Mozart and Haydn (Hide-n) give credit to C.P.E. (or "Cee" as I like to call him) for showing them the way. Really.

"Cee" or "Kee" (for K.P.E in German) wrote about nine hundred (!) Symphonies, Sonatas and other Songs.

Then he, like so many before him, promptly died (1788).

---

[*] More exciting factoids can be found in Appendix D. Exact dates are important only to statisticians and people who are, to put it clinically, "ac". (The "c" stands for compulsive.)

I'm thinking of calling my singing group *Buxtehude and the George Handels*.

Why are Music programs the first budget items that Public Schools cut?

From Bach to the Beatles – How Music Started

Another Scarlatti

One of the Scarlatti kids was an important "transition" composer. He also had 2 names: Giuseppe (Joe) and Dominico (not Joe).

"Joe" wrote 555 keyboard Sonatas, went to Portugal and Spain and experimented with "dissonances" (tones that sound "bad" to our ears because their vibrations "clash").

About 150 years later, the <u>Second Viennese School</u> with writers like Schönberg, Berg and Webern would experiment further with dissonances.

"Joe / not Joe" died in 1757 (or not).

Review Chapter 9 (or not).

Telemann and Gluck

Rounding out this bunch of friendly competitors were two Germans - G.P. Telemann (d. 1767) and C.W. Gluck (d. 1787).

Telemann wrote some three thousand musical pieces!

Gluck didn't.[*]

---

[*] More about Gluck in Opera, Chapter 19.

SORRY.

I INTERRUPT HERE FOR:

AN IMPORTANT DISCLAIMER!

My wife says I've been talking too much about composers dying.

Well, first, my friends, we must remind ourselves that we ALL DIE!

Second, I only began that in Chapter Nine.

She says that in Chapter 10, I appear to get into a "groove" and really get rolling in Chapter Eleven.

Well, OK.

In an effort to be NOT TOO morbid (And to Keep the Peace at home), I hereby resolve to approach the subject (Death) with more sympathy and delicacy.

In the next chapters, I shall attempt whole-heartedly to minimize these references.

Therefore, if any one of you readers starts to feel "dragged down" by incessant ponderings of your mortal doom, put that burden on yourself, not on me.

'Cause I done been pro-scribed to not do it NO MORE!

You - the reader - will judge whether this approach is or is not successful.

Thank you.

12. CLASSICAL (Part One)

Some people call ALL of this stuff "Classical" Music. Well, they are JUST FLAT WRONG!

Classical started when Franz Joseph Haydn started writing - about the time J.S. Bach die ...uh...passed away.

(I don't know if they PLANNED that or not.)

There wasn't much more folks could do with the "old" kinds of Music so they figured out some "new" kinds. Instruments became more important. (Voices, not-so-much.)

Music was beginning to follow certain Forms and Rules, which pretty much everybody used. (See Appendices C and D, for more about Musical Forms and Eras. It's sort of boring. Maybe you don't want to bother.)

Haydn

But back to Haydn (b. 1732 in Austria). When Franz was six, his parents shipped him out - for his own good - to live with a relative who could provide better Musical Training. He had two brothers who also got pretty good at Music.

Later, F.J. had a lousy marriage. I'll let each of you decide on his-or-her own whether you think Haydn's childhood affected his adulthood ...

From Bach to the Beatles – How Music Started

That sounds <u>ridiculous</u>.

<u>OF COURSE OUR CHILDHOOD AFFECTS OUR ADULTHOOD!</u>*

(What you see above is NOT a chapter heading, but rather a "trick" we writers sometimes use for emphasis.)

(Did I confuse you? Good.)

So, Franz - I call him Joe - got himself a regular job leading an Orchestra and he began writing Music.

He did a lot of it in places with names like Esterhazy, Eisenstadt and Eugene, which forces me to look up the spellings.

They are in Hungary, Austria and Botswana.

He worked for Princes called Paul Anton, Nikolaus and Little Kenny H.†

(See map on next page.)

---

* I'm sure many psychologists will back up this statement, if only for reasons of professional courtesy, right? Come on now, you psychologists . . . what do you say?

Question: Did Robin's <u>Hood</u> affect Little Red Riding's <u>Hood</u>?

There once was a Monk (munk) named <u>GUIDO</u>. Did you know that? He played an African Drum.

† It is alleged that Little Kenny H didn't come around much, due to the fact he wasn't going to be born yet for about 200 years.

From Bach to the Beatles – How Music Started

Can you believe this is still <u>Chapter 12</u>?

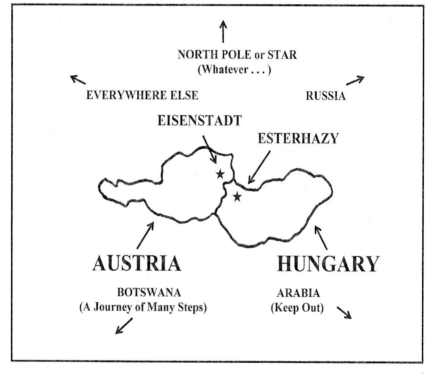

Haydn was the first-and-mostest creator of String Quartets.*

He wrote over 70 String Quartets, the most ever in the history of the Composers' League - to be surpassed only in 1927 by Babe Ruth with 60 (Home Runs).

---

* See Appendix C.

F.J. experimented with other early forms including a Stabat Mater.

Haydn (Hide-n) literally invented the Symphony.*

In one ten-year period, he set a WORLD'S RECORD for Symphonies, penning 40.

Franz ended up with 104 Symphonies - yet another RECORD, before slowing down in his "declining" years.

After 1809, he "declined" interviews, Tootsie Rolls and Verbs.

The main reason for this was because he was dea ...uh... deceased.

F.J. is known as "Papa" Haydn, not because he had kids (he had NOT), but because:

- he developed many Classical Music forms,
- he was a friend to Mozart,
- he taught Beethoven,
- it sounds cool,
- he was an all-around-good-guy ... and
- he was THE OLDEST!

---

* For more on the Symphony, see Appendix C and maybe also D or J. For Stabat Mater, see Appendix B and / or the Glossary.

13. CLASSICAL (Part Two)

The other two of the Big 3 Classical composers, besides Haydn, were Mozart (Moats-art) and Beethoven (Bay-toe-venn).

I've already mentioned them but there's more.

Mozart

Wolfgang Amadeus Mozart, (or as I call him, Mozart), was born in Salzburg, Austria and lived only 35 years. But he packed a heck-uv-a-lot into those years.

He was quite the "Ladies' Man" but as far as we know he had only one wife.

W.A. "dinked around" on the Piano at an early age (4), amazing his father and older sister Nannerl.

In 1772, Father Mozart took them both on a Performance Tour of Europe. Nan and "Little Wolf" were 9 and 6.

They went as far as Paris and London and the Tour lasted 3-and-a-half years!

In London, they met C.P.E. (or K.P.E.) Bach. (Remember good ol' "Cee"?) When they returned to Austria, the kids were 12 and 9 and had made the musical world a Whole Lot Richer.

From Bach to the Beatles – How Music Started

Mozart's writing career of about 30 years left us 30 Piano Concertos (some of the best ever), around forty String Quartets and Quintets (for 5 strings), 41 full Symphonies, a Requiem (largely unfinished), eighteen Masses, and 20 Operas![*]

<u>Starts with B</u>

Historians have discovered a "trend" of at least one Composer in each Era having a last name starting with "B". (This could be almost as exciting as the <u>*Da Vinci Code*</u> – or not.)

Back in Merry Old England, during the <u>Renascimento,</u> (look it up!) there was William Byrd. We visited him in Chapter 7.

There had been Bach (and the other Bach). Now there was Beethoven, of course, then Berlioz and Brahms (just wait).

To be followed by Berg, Chuck Berry and the Beatles.

OK.

---

[*] See Appendix E for highlights of Mozart's productive musical life. See Appendix C for Musical Forms.

For Opera, see Chapter 19 and Appendix E.

See Appendix F for some amusing anecdotes. See Appendix I for Medieval Monks (munks).

Incidentally, the Music of Anton Eberl (d. 1807), another Austrian, is often mistaken for Mozart's, a high compliment indeed.

Beethoven

Beethoven showed up late - in Bonn, Germany in 1770. Mozart, age 14, and Haydn, 38 had a good head start on him.

> Insert here: A QUICK ASIDE.

You must have noticed by now that most of these famous Baroque and Classical composers seem to have had the good fortune to be born in Austria or Germany.

It also didn't hurt that Vienna, Austria was pretty much the Centre of the Musical World. (Europeans like to say "Centre".)

Everybody ended up there, except maybe "crazy" Charlie Pachelbel, who went to America in 1734. Why did he do that?

> End of QUICK ASIDE.

Ludwig van B. infused his Music with new ideas surrounding very simple themes (Melodies).

His very First Symphony starts with an unusual chord. In the famous Fifth Symphony, Movement 3 blends into 4.

Humor plays a part with Beethoven. There's the "screw up" in Symphony #3 (Movement 1) when the French Horn melody comes in "too early".

Some of his Symphonic Codas are comically long, especially the final Movement of the 8th Symphony.

From Bach to the Beatles – How Music Started

Van (Lewd-fig) had serious anger issues. (He was not "well-tempered" like J.S. Bach.) Folks liked or disliked him, tried to ignore him, put up with his tantrums - but none could dispute his originality.

Beethoven began losing his hearing at 26. He had to deal with this affliction for over thirty years.

At the 1824 premiere of his grand Ninth Symphony, Ludwig insisted on directing, although he could not hear the Music. He could only feel the vibrations.

The emotional nature of Beethoven's Music heralded the Era of Romantic composers.

Ludwig's passing marked a big change in musical development. His funeral procession in 1827 was attended by 20,000 Viennese.*

"Freude schöner Götterfunken, Tochter aus Elysium."

from

Beethoven's 9th Symphony (*Ode to Joy*)

---

* Appendix G has lots more about LvB's Music.

14. EVEN MORE CLASSICAL
(Please, enough!)

Boccherini (Bock-ker-eeny)

Luigi Boccherini (b. 1743) was Italian. He spent much of his adult life in Spain where he wrote mostly for Cello and Guitar.

One piece: *Musica notturna delle Strade di Madrid* translates to: "We're not in Kansas anymore, Toto".

(My Spanish is as good as my Italian or my Italian is as good as my Spanish - or the lesser of these two sums.)

Like Corelli's Music before him (See Chapter 10), Some of Luigi's Music was used In the Movie: *Master and Commander: The Far Side of the World*.

(The Italians are staging a strong, late-game rally in the competition for "Most Classical Era Composers" but they will still lose by a score of 4-2.)

Clementi

Muzio Clementi (b. 1752) was a great player of the Pianoforte (our Piano) - maybe the best ever. And he was …yes… another Italian.

Clementi's Music greatly influenced Beethoven and Mozart. They all lived about the same time.

Muzio wrote approximately 110 Piano Sonatas and spent the last sixty years of his life in England. He has been called "Father of the Piano(forte)".

On one Concert Tour of the continent, Clementi had the honor to play for Marie Antoinette, Queen of France – a few years BEFORE she had her head cut off.

Schubert

Franz Schubert (Shoe-bear-tt) of Austria was another Classical-to-Romantic Composer. (Transitional, like Beethoven.)

"Shoe" wrote over 1000 works of which six hundred or so were Songs.[*]

Franz (fronds) is also well known for a _Rosamunde Overture,_ based on a collection of incidental Music and for his "Unfinished" 8th Symphony.[†]

---

[*] Songs are sung with instrumental accompaniment, usually Piano. German speakers refer to these as Lieder (Lee-derr). See Mendelssohn, Schumann and and Brahms (coming up), plus Appendix C if you absolutely obsess on these sorts of things.

[†] PDQ Bach, a mostly fictional person who is still alive today, claims to have written an "Unbegun" Symphony. I'm not sure …

From Bach to the Beatles – How Music Started

"Shoe" also wrote a Stabat Mater, lots of chamber music, including several String Quartets, and some Piano pieces for four hands (although we're pretty sure that he, himself possessed only two ... hands).[*]

Schubert expired in 1828 at 31. He would have been the youngest, except for Pergolesi (see Chapter 10).

It might have been Typhoid Fever or a "social" disease that did him in. But either way ...

BULLETIN:

➢ Insert: REMINDER.

Due to a pledge I made earlier, please ignore any reference to the untimely ...uh... demise of Schubert or Pergolesi or Mozart.

We appreciate it.

➢ End of REMINDER.

Now we can finally move on to the Romantic Era.

---

[*] For Stabat Mater, see Appendix B. For hands, see "Christian Andersen."

African Drums were often hallowed logs - very religious.

Once I tried writing a "Semi-Opera" but I could only get half way through it.

Can you write a limerick starting with: "There once was a young Monk named Guido..."?

From Bach to the Beatles – How Music Started

15. HERE'S WHAT'S HAPPENING NEXT…

By now there were literally thousands of guys writing Music. They're only the ones we KNOW about!

> Insert: NOTE FOR FEMALE READERS.

It is apparent that <u>Feminine Inequality</u> DID NOT DIE OUT after the Dark Ages. Just so you know…

> End of NOTE FOR FEMALE READERS.

Thanks to Revolutions in the 1700s and 1800s (both military and industrial) more people had time and money to compose, instruments were built better and more folks could go to concerts.

Don't worry though. I couldn't dare cover all this - especially not in a chapter or two.

So I will "hit" on a couple of the "biggies" and, if you read kinda fast, we may just get through this, relatively unscathed.

Coming up is the <u>Romantic Era</u>. "Romantic" in Music Development does NOT refer to Lovey-Dovey or Kissy-Kissy stuff.

That's all well and good to a purpose, but we're not here to mess around. We're here to have a GOOD TIME, by Jove (whoever Jove is).

16. ROMANTIC - EARLY (First Love)

I've already said Beethoven and Schubert are called the first Romantics (gradual change from Classical, more emotion).*

There follows a virtual flood of Romantics slopping over into the 20th Century. I've split this up into four chapters: Early Romantic, Middle Romantic, Later Romantic and Opera.

Each Chapter is as short as I can make it. I don't want to get bored, either.

Paganini

First on the non-boring Romantic list is - (are you ready for this?) - an Italian! Violinist *extraordinaire* Niccolo Paganini was born in 1782 in Genoa, home town of Cristoforo Colombo.

Some of you may know this historic giant as Christopher Columbus - founder of the Cincinnati Reds baseball team.

Actually, being born in Genoa, his Genoese name was Christoffa Corombo. (You have to say it with a lisp.)

I'll bet you didn't even know there WAS such a language as Genoese (neither did I).

---

* There's a good discussion about Emotion in Music in Appendix H. I know it's good because it came from my very own brain.

From Bach to the Beatles – How Music Started

The Ships of Christoffa Corombo

El Nino   Santa Anita

Pinto Bean

But back to Niccolo …

Paganini wrote his own Music, mostly for Violin. He was friends with Berlioz (we'll meet him next) and Rossini (wait until Opera).

Later Composers arranged and adapted much of Paganini's Music. Among them were Lizq#s?t, Schumann, Brahms, Rachmaninoff and Andrew Lloyd Webber.[*]

Nick (Pags) and Chris (Corombo) never met. That's because Columbus had been "pushing up daisies" for about 275 years.

(See? Most demurely spoke!)

---

[*] These guys are listed elsewhere in this Amazing Musical Tome. See the Index for more – if you dare. For Tome, see Glossary.

Berlioz

Which brings us to Hector Berlioz (Bear-lee-oh-z). Yes. Hector. A perfectly fine French name. He was born in 1803.

"Heck" was mainly an Orchestra conductor who loved leading large Orchestras – like 1,000 or so musicians playing in front of thousands of people in an audience. (Normal size for an Orchestra was 30-50 members.)

Berlioz wrote an Opera and, like Mozart, a Requiem.*

His Requiem was called: <u>Une Grande Messe des Mortres</u> which means: "A Large Launch of Artillery Shells".

Hector read some Shakespeare and created a "Dramatic" Symphony based on the play Romeo and Juliet.

But good ol' "Heck" was more famous for 2 other things.

First, Berlioz wrote a 5-movement Symphony only three years after Beethoven's deat …uh… departure called <u>Symphonie Fantastique</u> (1830). Movements 1-4 are "normal". The 5th is, to put it mildly, bizarre!†

---

* A Requiem is a Church Service for the Dead. See Forms in Appendix C.

† This movement is called "Witches' Sabbath". It is a wild dance and includes the <u>Dies Irae</u> (Day of Wrath) theme from Medieval times. That theme was designed to scare the holy you-know-what out of the faithful church-goer, driving him to drink or become a Monk (munk), whichever sum is greater. This explains our present-day title "The Grapes of Wrath". Glory Hallelujah!

The second thing Berlioz did? He hatched a plot to kill his fiancée, her mother and her new intended - after she broke off her engagement to good, normal run-of-the-mill Hector.

He was to wear a disguise and use pistols (with poison as a back up). But Berlioz didn't "seal the deal" because he left part of his disguise on a train! What the "Heck".

Did I mention he was French?

We really need to "git along little dogies" and finish off the Early Romantics. So…

Mendelssohn

Jakob Ludwig Felix Mendelssohn was a German composer (b. 1809). He sometimes added the last name Bartholdy (I might have chosen something spicier).

Mendelssohn was a Conductor and Pianist. He also wrote a lot (about 560 Pieces) – including some which could be classified as Lieder (Lee-derr) – just as his contemporaries Schubert and Schumann and (a little later) Brahms.

An Overture called *A Midsummer Night's Dream* is, again, based on a Shakespeare play.

Mendelssohn later added a famous "Wedding March" to the *Dream* which thousands of people still march to today – at Ship Christenings and Ice Cream Socials.

Felix's Symphonies were numbered 1, 5, 4, 2 and 3. He also wrote 3 Oratorios (Oreos) and lived many years in England and Scotland. There he got to meet Queen Victoria and Prince Albert.

Mendelssohn lived only 38 years. Queen Victoria reigned over Britain for about 63 years. She wins.

Chopin

Frederic Chopin (pronounced like the French) was Polish - no joke - (b. 1810), but he quickly went to Paris. His Piano Music requires great manual dexterity and good hands – usually two.

Mendelssohn, Berlioz and Lizq#s?t (don't worry, he's next) were friends with Chopin in France. Chopin (Show-pahhnnn) wrote mostly Piano Music and mostly for himself.

His best known piece is the *Minute Waltz*, which actually takes about a minute and 43 seconds.

1:43

"Fred" also wrote:

- 27 études (which means "study" in French),
- 25 préludes (meaning "coming before something else") and
- 0 "Hey, Dudes!" (having to do with Rap Music, which this author does NOT cover in this or ANY book.)

Frederic was sickly most of his life. But he never lost his sense of humor.

Once, while recuperating on the Island of Majorca (My-york-uh) in the Mediterranean Sea, with his "girlfriend" George Sand, Chopin seemed to be very frustrated at being sick so much of the time.*

Fred tells the following tale on himself:

He visited 3 Doctors.

The first Doc told him he would die soon; the second said he was on his last breath; and the third Doctor told him he was ALREADY DEAD!

(Oh, those wacky Romantic Composers.)

Chopin did di …uh… pass on, unfortunately, at age 39.

---

* Despite the name, G.S. was female. If you're older than 11, change "girlfriend" to read "mistress".

Lizq#s?t

Franz Lizq#s?t (b. 1811) was a Hungarian Pianist. His father worked for the Esterhazys in Austria / Hungary / Botswana (See Chapter 12).

Daddy Lizq#s?t knew Haydn (Hide-n) pretty well and also Beethoven. So, obviously "little Frankie" grew up musically advantaged, one could say.

Lizq#s?t (pronounced Lizq#s?t) spent time in Paris and was friends with Chopin (See last section).

Franz (Fronds) arranged hundreds of Musical pieces for other writers.

He did manage to compose some pieces for himself. His works include nine Symphonic Poems and 19 Hungarian Rhapsodies. Rhapsody number Two is pretty famous.

There's more about Lizq#s?t … uh …"Fronds" way up ahead in Chapter 18, when we talk about Edvard Grieg.

This involves a Hungarian meeting a Norwegian in Rome, Italy. Say, what? (I'll bet you just can't wait.)

Franz had trouble spelling his name, as did some of his relatives, namely Christmas, Shopping and Laundry.

(I just could not resist.)

From Bach to the Beatles – How Music Started

Schumann

Born in Germany in 1810, Robert Schumann soon married Clara. She was a fine Pianist and helped his career, both musically and business-wise.

Robert was famous for his <u>Lieder</u> (Lee-derr). Surely you remember from Chapter 14 and earlier in this chapter that <u>Lieder</u> (Lee-derr) are simply Songs sung in German. Refer to the sections on Schubert and Mendelssohn.

And stop calling me Shirley.

(I'm certain there will be more about <u>Lieder</u> (Lee-derr) as we delve further into the bowels of this epistle. You know me ...)

Schumann also wrote one Opera and 4 Symphonies.

Robert and Clara had a good marriage, but then Robert started hearing "things" - real (tinnitus) and imagined (angel voices).

He tried jumping into the Rhine River only to be rescued by boatmen. He then had himself committed as insane and for the final two years of his life was not able to see his beloved wife Clara.

Very tragic. He di ...uh... became bereft of life at 46.

Good friend Johannes Brahms comforted Clara and helped spread Robert's good name and Music. For this, Brahms gets his own section.

17. ROMANTIC - MIDDLE (Net Serve)

These next guys belong in the Romantic Era because they were born then. Also Music was expressing more feelings.*

Brahms

Johannes Brahms (b. 1833) spent much of his childhood in Hamburg, a harbor city. Hamburg's "Hafen" is huge! This author had the privilege of touring it some years ago.

The Brahms family was poor. Johannes learned Piano from his father and by playing at taverns and brothels.

His experiences with the rowdiness of drunken sailors affected his Music and – some say - his emotional well being.

Brahms was 20 when he met the Schumanns. Robert died about three years later, leaving Johannes to look after Clara.

"Joe" devoted himself to popularizing Robert's Music and Clara's piano playing.

Clara was older then Brahms and it is unclear exactly what their relationship was.

But, whatever, "Joe" stood by her.†

---

* Appendix H has all the "skinny" about Romantic Era Music.

† Please see the last part of Chapter 16 for more about Robert, Clara and Johannes.

From Bach to the Beatles – How Music Started

Brahms' compositions include works for just about every instrument and every Form. He wrote for small groups, soloists and large Orchestras (Including four Symphonies).

A German Requiem is a famous large work by Brahms for Choir, soloists and Orchestra. I got to sing it in college.

As did his friend Robert Schumann and Mendelssohn and Schubert before them, "Joe" composed hundreds of Songs – to be sung in German and thereby labeled Lieder (Lee-derr).[*]

In 1897, Brahms dy …uh… succumb …uh… joined the "choir invisible".

History mentions Johannes Brahms as one of The 3 B's greatest composers (along with Bach and Beethoven).[†]

The Russians are coming!

The Russians are coming!

---

[*] This is becoming tiresome. If you absolutely need to research these Songs further, look at the Composers mentioned (see Glossary) and in Appendix C. And DO NOT bother me about this again, Okay?

[†] The 3 B's are called the greatest primarily because they contributed so much to Music, especially Counterpoint and Development. There's an attempt to explain in Appendix J. You may want to wear hip boots 'cause it gets pretty deep in there. Also, see the Glossary.

From Bach to the Beatles – How Music Started

The Russians are here!

The Russians are here!

Pyotr Ilyich Tchaikovsky

Now, do you feel better? We've gotten away from all those Italians and Austrians and Germans. And we only had to GO TO RUSSIA to do it!

Tchaikovsky (Chigh-koff-ski) felt at home in St. Petersburg. He traveled extensively and was well aware of what was happening musically in Europe.

His Music follows the "Western" tradition - more so than the "Russian Five" who tried to go in different directions.[*]

Pyotr (Pete) was often severely depressed. Most of his life he didn't seem to fit in. His mother died when he was a teenager. He married later in life and it was a disaster. He was never self-assured about many aspects of his life and lifestyle.

So, you'd think his Music would be really sad and yucky.

No way!

---

[*] The Five were Stasov, Balakirev, Cui, Rimsky-Korsakov, Borodin and Mussorgsky. (That's 6, but oh well…)

From Bach to the Beatles – How Music Started

Oh sure, some of his Music is sad. It can run the gamut of emotions. Much of it is beautiful. Parts can become thrillingly loud. That's why we call it Romantic.*

There are at least three ways Tchaikovsky (b. 1840) excelled musically:

- He wrote some captivating melodies,
- His use of instrument combinations is often inspired and unique, and
- He was a master at "building tension." (Like starting really low and soft and only gradually bringing the Music to an over-the-top climactic moment.)†

Yeah, I'm a fan.

Pete was a child genius. He knew French and German by age 6 and played a mean Piano by age eight. They say.

Tchaikovsky wrote six complete Symphonies, 11 Operas, an _1812 Overture_, three Ballets, quite a bit of Piano Music and much more.‡

---

* In addition to beautiful tunes, Pete uses Tympani extensively. They are Drums. It may be that they came from Africa …

† For more about "tension and release" and other fascinating tidbits about Romantic Music, see Appendix H and, after your snack, maybe J.

‡ Tchaikovsky's Ballets - _Swan Lake_, _Sleeping Beauty_ and the _Nutcracker_ - are all very well known.

From Bach to the Beatles – How Music Started

After Beethoven, Pyotr Ilyich is the second most popular composer in the U.S. and Great Britain.

He was guest conductor at the opening of Carnegie Hall in New York (1891).

Pete's …uh… lease on life expired two years later. Some suspect suicide. Very sad.[*]

Hanging around Russia a bit longer we just may run into:

Nikolai Rimsky-Korsakov

Born near St. Petersburg in 1844, R-K joined the Russian Navy at 18. He managed to pursue this early career and continue to compose Music. Rimsky-Korsakov literally "saw the world" visiting ports like London, Rio de Janeiro and Niagara Falls (?).

Back in Russia Nicolai married Nadezhda and they had seven children. Their marriage was not unlike the Schumanns, Robert and Clara.[†]

Nadezhda (try spelling THAT several times!) helped Nick musically as well as with the business end of Music writing.

---

[*] Sometime, you should listen to the *Nutcracker Suite*, just to check out the incredible variety of instruments Tchaikovsky used!

[†] See Schumanns at the end of Chapter 16.

From Bach to the Beatles – How Music Started

At 27, R-K was a "diamond in the rough". He was a natural, instinctive writer, but knew little about composing traditions. He learned, even while teaching, at the St. Petersburg Conservatory.

Lots of notable composers studied under Rimsky-Korsakov at St. Petersburg. Most famous were Stravinsky, Prokofiev and Respighi.

"Nick" is considered a member of the "Russian Five".[*] This group tried to distance itself from traditional "Western" Music. Nikolai managed somewhere in between.

Folk subjects and Fairy Tales, both Russian and foreign dot his Music. Examples?

- *Capriccio Espagnol,*
- *Fantasia on Serbian Themes,*
- *Russian Easter Festival Overture,*
- *Flight of the Bumblebee* and
- *Scheherazade.*

All these pieces show exotic use of Melody, Harmony and Rhythm.[†]

---

[*] For more on The "Russian" Five, go back three pages, Do-Not-Pass-Go, Do-Not-Collect-200-Rupees ...

[†] Remember these VIPs from early on in Chapters 2, 3 and 4?

From Bach to the Beatles – How Music Started

Rimsky-Korsakov's musical legacy includes a dozen-or-so Operas, 20 choral pieces and another 20 large orchestral works. Two-and-a-half of these are Symphonies (Numbers 1 and 3 as well as half of number 2).

Finally in 1908, Nicolai …uh… stopped because his heart already had (!?)

Now, with permission, I will revert to the German-Austrian groups, just for a moment. It's for a good purpose.

Ladies and Gentlemen, we are pleased to introduce, on the next page, the Waltz King himself:

Johann Strauss, Jr.

Johann Baptist, Johann the Younger, Johann, Jr., Joe the Second and Johann Sohn (son) are all the same guy.

That's to distinguish him from his Father, who was already famous in Vienna.

Johann Senior said "no" to his sons' studying Music, even to beating them.

Only when father abandoned the family could Josef, Eduard and "Junior" comfortably pursue their Music.

Strauss Jr.'s Music is light, danceable - not a lot of "heavy" stuff like Symphonies.

Prima Specie is the Waltz.*

There are over a hundred of his Waltzes. Many are performed at the January 1st "Neujahrskonzert" in Vienna. The program is telecast worldwide. Donna and I never miss it!

Johann the Son's most popular set of Waltzes is *An der schönen blauen Donau* (The famous "Blue Danube").

Alongside the Waltzes, Joe the Second wrote around 100 Polkas and Marches.

---

* Waltzes are always written in three-quarter time, i.e. 3 beats to a measure, moderate speed, therefore you can easily dance to them. In the late 1800s Waltzes were new, scandalous and sensational. People danced together: holding each other. Unheard of.

From Bach to the Beatles – How Music Started

Brothers Josef and Eduard also had good musical successes.

Strauss Jr. clocked in with 15 Operettas. These are full-blown theater works, like Opera, but actors are allowed to talk between Songs.*

These Operettas are old-fashioned to many but they are still fun to enjoy. Especially *der Zigeunerbaron* ("Gypsy Baron") and *die Fledermaus* ("the Bat").

Fledermaus has some VERY funny stuff in it. And you can sometimes catch it in an English translation, if you want to. I prefer the German, because I can understand most of it.

(I'm not bragging, just stating a fact. It's for darn sure my German is better than the other languages I tout that I "know".)

Johann the Younger married 3 times. Not simultaneously, thank goodness, and not to the same woman!

He and his Music were admired by Richard Wagner and Richard Strauss (no relation to Eduard, Joseph or Johann).†

Joe Jr. d …uh… "bought the farm" in 1899.

---

* For more on Opera, see Chapter 19, Appendix C and Book II.

There's a lot more about Operettas in Part II of this impossibly fabulous Fount of Knowledge. Go buy a copy right away… today…NOW!

† Richard Wagner is not pronounced the way it looks in "American". The Germanic is Ree-kard Vawg-nerr. (See Wagner in Chapter 19, Opera.)

For more about Richard Strauss, that's also in Book II. Buy one, OK?

18. ROMANTIC - LATER (Foot Fault)

Dvorak

Antonin Leopold Dvorak was born in 1841 in what was part of Czechoslovakia that actually belonged to Austria back then.

He had two funny "gidgets" over the R and A in his last name, which I guess tells you to pronounce it Dee-vor-zhawk.

Tony spent plenty of time abroad – In England, Russia and even America for three years.

In the States, he got a feel for some of our folk Music and used it in his famous 9th Symphony, titled: *From the New World*.

He was influenced strongly by Beethoven, Schubert, Wagner and List … Lizts … Lizq#s?t …uh … the guy who wrote the Hungarian Rhapsodies.*

Dvorak played Keyboard and Violin (+ Viola). Native Slavic themes dotted his works, most of which he wrote in Czechoslovakia. (Czechoslovakia is now split into two countries.)

Tony married later in life (at 32) and still had time to produce nine kids.

---

* "L….. " (The Hungarian Rhapsody guy) – Since we cannot even spell his name, we cannot be held accountable to pronounce it.

From Bach to the Beatles – How Music Started

We inherit from Dvorak a large body of Music including nine Symphonies (like Beethoven), 16 Operas, a dozen-or-so String Quartets, 4 Concerti (that's more than one Kon-chair-toe), two Masses, a Requiem and a Stabat Mater.*

A.L. Dvorak left us (to struggle ahead alone, without him) in 1904.

Coming up: Norway (oh, boy)!

Grieg

Notice we're venturing away from the German-Austrian-Italian core zone? Seems only fair.

Next we have the one-and-only Edvard Hagerup Grieg. Edvard (Eddie) Hagerup (Batter up!) was born in Norway in 1843.

Cold it was, too, I am told - although it was June.

Grieg is famous for a Piano Concerto and a Suite (Sweet) of pieces based on Peer (or Per) Gynt.

<u>Gynt</u> is a Norwegian fairy tale about a no-good mischief-maker. <u>In the Hall of the Mountain King</u> from the <u>Peer Gynt Suite</u> is famous, even if Ed Haggy (Grieg) did not like it much.

---

* For Stabat Mater, see Appendix B.

Leonard Bernstein wrote a Mass in the 1950s. He uses <u>actual swear words</u> in it!

From Bach to the Beatles – How Music Started

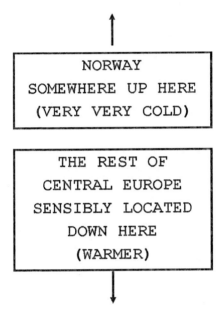

Grieg was once actually <u>Greig</u> (Greg). His ancestors came over from Scotland. Aye.

See? That's what's wrong with the World.

You take a guy from Scotland, move him to Norway and foul up a beautiful pure language with stuff like MacNamara and Kilts and Scotch!

Norwegian used to be so easy, with all those umlauts.[*]

---

[*] Answer to riddle: because it was stapled to the Chicken!

From Bach to the Beatles – How Music Started

Ed married and had a child who unfortunately did not survive past age two.

One time Grieg visited his friend Franz Li … (Hungarian Rhapsody guy) in Rome. (That's in Italy.)

Grieg brought with him Piano Concerto Music and Lizq#s?t sight read it!

Folks, that ain't easy to do – and he (the "L…" guy) also played the Orchestra part on the Piano!

People say Clementi (Chapter 14) or Chopin (Chapter 16) were the best on Keyboard, but "L…" was pretty sensational.

I was not there to judge, but … hey.

Grieg's legacy includes one Symphony and hundreds of songs and dances, mostly for Piano and Voice and based on Norwegian folk lore.

Grieg "departed" this planet in 1907.

Mahler

I don't know much about Gustav Mahler (Mm-aah-lerr), so maybe we can learn together.

Mahler, like Dvorak, was born in part of Czechoslovakia, which belonged to Austria. His family was Jewish and not rich, which in those times (1860) meant problems of social stigma.

From Bach to the Beatles – How Music Started

Still, Mahler's father managed to get him into the Vienna Music Conservatory. He found success as an Orchestra Conductor.

Through a series of conducting positions Gus wound up at the Vienna Hof Opera.

Along the way he got himself "converted" to Catholicism, perhaps mostly to obtain jobs.

Late in life, he also had some success in New York with the Philharmonic and the Metropolitan Opera (the "Met").

Some folks call Mahler the "greatest" conductor of Wagner and Mozart Operas.

Even as he was busy conducting Operas, Mahler managed to compose dozens of songs.

Notably Gus used several Folk Poems from a series: <u>Des Knabben Wunderhorn</u> ("Knobby and his Magic Banana"). Some are sung and played individually. Others are incorporated into his Symphonies, which total 9 and ½ (incomplete #10).

Mahler often had difficulties with his Orchestra personnel and with critics. He was apparently a dictatorial conductor and a tough task master.

His performances were sometimes criticized and even belittled. His use of a "square" drum in Symphony # 6 added to his reputation as an eccentric.[*]

---

[*] Perhaps this was because the drum came from Africa. I really don't know.
If that drum was carved out of a <u>tree</u>, did it have a <u>square root</u>?

From Bach to the Beatles – How Music Started

Gus married late (42) and had two daughters. One died young. The other was a well-known sculptor and lived until 1988.

Some notable Mahler followers established a <u>Second Viennese School</u>. Three mainstays were Schönberg, Berg and Webern.

These guys were at the leading edge of a movement called "Atonality" (where the musical key you are in doesn't really matter).

Similar attempts were happening in England and America. That type of music is not especially this writer's "cup of tea".

Mahler's Music lapsed into obscurity after his corporeal demise in 1911.

Partly responsible was the rise to power of Hitler and the Nazis' anti-semitism.

In the 1950s, Mahler's fame was restored - largely thanks to the efforts of the U.S.'s Leonard Bernstein.

Debussy

Claude Debussy (b. 1862) was French and an "impressionist" like the painters Monet, Manet and Renoir.

Much of his Music describes what Springtime or Moonlight or Dead Leaves or Flapjacks or the Sea might "sound like".

In this pursuit, Claude uses "odd" devices like Pentatonic or Whole Tone scales.*

Not surprisingly his works are titled Fantasies, Rhapsodies, Reveries, Chansons, Regrets, Romances, Ballads and Nom-de-plumes (Plumb-de-booms).

These Forms musically express things and feelings. When Debussy builds up tension, it doesn't always release "pleasantly" to our ears. His Music is an acquired taste.†

Claude wrote a couple hundred pieces mostly for Piano and Voice. He was an excellent Pianist. That's what I heard, anyway.

Debussy also composed chamber music, four Ballets and six larger orchestral works including one Opera.

Claude was truly a "Ladies' Man" like Mozart before him. He did marry, but in five years divorced and re-married. He had only one child, a daughter.

Debussy spent some time in Germany learning and liking Wagner Opera.

He lived four years in Rome where he saw Italian Opera but did not like it - or Rome - very much.

---

* Claude (Klo-d) often uses Pentatonic (5-note) and Whole Tone (6) scales instead of the usual Octave (7-note) scale. The resulting Harmonies are "strange".

† For more about dissonance and tension and release, see Chapter 11 (Scarlatti), Chapter 16 (Tchaikovsky) and Appendix H.

From Bach to the Beatles – How Music Started

Claude "ceased to live" in 1918 as the Germans were bombarding Paris near the end of World War I.*

His daughter survived him, but only until 1919.

Ravel

Maurice Ravel was French like Debussy, an impressionist like Debussy, and, although twelve years younger and destined to live 18 years longer, he was a friend of Debussy.

Debussy was also a friend to Ravel.

They both liked Stravinsky (see Book II), who also hung out in Paris those days and who also liked them.

Get it? Got it. Good!†

To call Ravel simply an impressionist is too limiting.

His Music often shows "Modern" and even "Classical" elements. So he is a unique "transitional" composer with broader composing abilities than others.

Also gifted at the Piano, "Mo's" forte (pun only slightly intended) was orchestration and arranging.

---

* None of this is very amusing – certainly not the dying or War parts. Hey ... this reporter tells it like it is. We can't ALWAYS be hilarious.

† This is, of course, a quote from that riotous Movie: <u>The Court Jester</u>, starring the incomparable Danny Kaye.

From Bach to the Beatles – How Music Started

Most notable Ravel arrangement: Modest Mussorgsky's *Pictures at an Exhibition*.

Pictures is a Piano Suite (Sweet) in ten movements written by Mussorgsky, a Russian, based on an exhibit of paintings by Viktor Hartmann in St. Petersburg in 1874.

The Ravel orchestral arrangement stands above others, due to the especial "timbre" or colorings he used.[*]

Ravel wrote another piece: *Le Tombeau de Couperin* ("Couperin Falls Off The Parallel Bars"). This was written – painstakingly – in its entirety, on Couperin's body cast . . . as a tribute to that composer's gymnastic prowess. Or not.

Ravel's best known work is *Bolero*, written after the War (1928).

"Mo" didn't like his creation, calling it a composition "without development".

---

[*]Timbre (Tam-burr) refers to the unique sounds you can get from a particular instrument. An oboe, for example, can sound "rounded", almost like an echo, but can also be harsh, as maybe a Chicken squawking as it carries a Caterpillar across the road, stapled to it.

An expert can figuratively "paint" a picture and that's what Ravel does – musically paint Hartmann's ten *Pictures* based on Mussorgsky's Piano compositions. It's good stuff. Listen sometime.

This musical term is not to be confused with the yell used by lumberjacks when felling a tree in the woods. By the way, if there's nobody there to hear it, does the falling tree make a sound? Also, not to be used as in the sentence: "Don't timbre with the U.S. mail. You know it's a Federal Offense."

There's speculation that <u>Bolero</u> was influenced by <u>frontotemporal dementia</u> developing in Ravel's brain.

I'm serious here, believe it or not.

Brain damage sustained in a Paris Taxi accident (1932) further limited him.

(This author can personally testify to the dangers of Parisian traffic!)

<u>Paris Taxi</u> (very dangerous!)

From Bach to the Beatles – How Music Started

In 1984's Winter Olympic Games held in Sarajevo (Capital City of Bosnia and Herzegovina), England's Jayne Torvill and Christopher Dean ice danced to Ravel's *Bolero* for a most famous and excellent "perfect" event.*

Look it up on YouTube. It's amazing!

A 1928 tour of the U.S. included "Mo's" meeting American Jazz legends George Gershwin and Duke Ellington.

Upon Ravel's ...uh... ethereal departure (1937), he left us with two Ballets, 1 Opera and about a hundred other pieces.

A PENULTIMATE NOTE

This almost concludes the Romantic Era (hooray). Only two chapters remain: Opera and Coming Attractions.

If I were you (and who's to say I'm not?) I'd run right out and buy From Bach to the Beatles, Part II. And, if you can't find it, harass your local Book Dealer Person until he-or-she gets you a copy.

(You could also wait until the book is written ...)

---

* Back then, Sarajevo was an important city in Yugoslavia. But then that Country broke up into lots of little countries and that's how we find things in our ever-increasingly political World of today. As the Song says: *Breaking up is hard to do.*

19. OPERA (Not-My-Fault)

There is way too much Opera to cover in one chapter.

You Opera lovers will be saddened by omissions, but be heartened to know I present a broad outline.

If you're not so much interested in Opera, (1) maybe you should be and / or (2) it'll be pretty swift and painless.

If you've faithfully read the previous 18 chapters, you will NOT be at all surprised when I tell you Opera developed in ... here we go again ... Italy!

Opera is (as solemnly declared in Appendix C) a musical Story with staging for Voices and Instruments, to be acted out.

You may quote me.

The Story part is called the Libretto (Stoh-ree).

The musical part is called the Music (the good-sounds-happening-together part).

Somebody named Jacopo Peri wrote an Opera called *Dafne* in 1598 in Florence, northern Italy. It got lost.

But the idea spread – first throughout Italy, then to the rest of Europe.

Most folks would agree that Italy is still the primo country for Opera.

From Bach to the Beatles – How Music Started

➢ V.I.I.N. (Very Important and Informative Note):

It is far too easy to "slough off" Opera as high brow, heavy or (God forbid) boring.

Don't do that!

This author-person pleads guilty to doing some of that once-upon-a-time-ago and he regretted it. It cost several years of getting to know SOME really good Music. So, let's be fair. Start with an Overture or two (maybe Rossini) and give Opera a chance.

I thank you. Lincoln Center thanks you. Sydney thanks you (and stop calling me Shirley).

➢ End of V.I.I.N.

Now, back to our story…

The World's most famous Opera house is La Scala in Milan, northern Italy.

Other well-known Opera houses include the Paris Opera, the New York Metropolitan (The "Met"), the Vienna State Opera, London's Royal Opera and the Peoria Back Alley Song Shack.

There is one Opera house built basically for Richard Wagner alone – the Festspielhaus in Bayreuth, Germany.[*]

* * *

---

[*] These are just the "top" spots. Others would argue the quality of Opera "homes" in Sydney, Berlin, Dresden, the Kennedy Center in Washington, D.C., the handful in Russia or dozens of others around the planet. Look one up nearest to you! And please don't argue.

From Bach to the Beatles – How Music Started

"Comic", "Serious", "More Serious", "Grand" and "Soap" are Opera classifications.

Terms like <u>Buffa,</u> <u>Seria,</u> <u>Bel Canto,</u> <u>Reform,</u> <u>Verismo</u> and <u>Grand</u> (yeah, same word) are appropriate adjectives to be looked up in your Funk and Wagnalls.

An Overture begins the Opera. But the main rocket in Opera's arsenal is the <u>Aria</u>. This is simply a Song. The lead actors get to sing at least one of these per show.

The other actor / singers get to stand around and sing chorus. Whoopee.

("Hey, Georgio – let's go get a Beer and watch some Fuchsias grow!")[*]

Opera is completely sung. (I'll bet you already knew that.) There's no talking. So the in-between parts of the Libretto are sung in <u>Recitative</u> style. It's like talking with a simple melodic line.[†]

This method advances the Story and leads to another Aria, or to the occasional duet / trio, or to a hideous death scene where somebody gets stabbed or poisoned. They sing that part, too!

Most Opera is written in Italian. Now this may seem like a "duh!" moment to some of you, but it's *de rigueur mortis* ("over my dead body") to study Opera in Italy.

---

[*] See Babylon, Chapter 3.

[†] <u>Recitative</u> is pronounced Ress-i-tah-teev (accent on the "eev").

From Bach to the Beatles – How Music Started

Opera – Early Roots

Allesandro Scarlatti (see Chapter 9) wrote about 60 Operas through the early 1700s. Titles such as:

O cessate di piagarmi ("Oh, quit your belly-aching!") and *Toglietemi la vita ancor* ("Toss Timmy Overboard the Anchor") improved to later ones like:

Il triono dell'onore ("The Troublesome Tricycle") and *Griselda* - really!

* * *

Antonio Vivaldi (also Chapter 9) said he wrote 94 Operas. Fifty have been identified and about twenty survive. One of his works is:

La virtu trionfante dell'amore, e dell'odio, overo il Tigrane

("Winning True Love produces a Thunderous Headache"). Also, two are about Forida:

Orlando finto pazzo and *Orlando furioso,*

("Finding good Italian Food at Disney World while not getting angry"),

and there's a *Griselda*.

Copycat.

From Bach to the Beatles – How Music Started

In Germany, Heinrich Schütz supposedly wrote the first German Opera, called <u>Dafne</u> (just like Peri's earlier in this chapter) and it got lost (also just like Peri's). This was in the 1620s.

He also managed to write his "swan song" – in fact 13 of them. They had titles like:

<u>Zeige mir, Herr, den Weg deiner Rechte</u>

("Sir, I'm from Australia; we drive on the left"), and

<u>Ich hasse die Flattergeister</u>

("I don't like Spiders and Snakes").

* * *

Maybe we'll have better luck in England.

Early Opera efforts in jolly old Britain were exerted by Henry Purcell (Chapter 9) and his teacher, John Blow. (I swear by Dave Barry, I am not making this up.)

Blow wrote <u>Venus and Adonis</u> while Purcell wrote <u>Dido and Aeneas</u> (who are not the same two people). These Operas appeared in the late 1600s.

Purcell's experimenting with Opera included his coming up with the concept of a Semi-Opera. I have already said that a Semi-Opera is not only a vague concept, undoubtedly half-baked, but also possibly baloney.*

---

* Baloney hails from Bologna, Italy, which sort of takes us full circle, doesn't it? However, we are not through with Opera just yet, so hang on.

<u>Bologna, Italy around 1700.</u>

The Roots of early Opera include:
- Handel's 40-some (England),
- Mozart's twenty or so (Austria) and
- Beethoven's one-and-only *Fidelio* (Germany).

See Chapters 9 and 13.

In addition, early English attempts included Thomas Arne's (1710-1778) Operas and other dramatic varieties - numbering several dozen - along with Purcell's efforts (see above).

In France Jean-Baptiste Lully, the aptly named "father" of French Opera (d. 1687) wrote 14 of them.

Rameau (French, Chapter 10, d. 1764) composed about thirty Operas and Ballets.

Soon others were angling away from Italian-only Opera. They include:

- Carl Maria von Weber (1786-1826) of northern Germany, who wrote a half dozen Operas, paving the way for German Romantics, especially Wagner,
- C.W. Gluck (d. 1787), a German who had some Libretti written in French as well as Italian (but NOT German!),
- Richard Wagner (German, d. 1883) and
- Georges Bizet (French, d. 1875).

Opera – Sprouting Branches

Opera was everywhere in Romantic Europe of the 1800s.

First there was the <u>Bel Canto</u> period, comprising the group of Vincenzo Bellini (b. 1801), Gaetano Donizetti (b. 1797) and Gioachino Rossini (b. 1792) – all Italian, as if that's a surprise.[*]

<u>Bel Canto</u> means "beautiful singing" but the term has changed over the years. Maybe "smooth lyrical musical lines" would describe it better.

In some ways it was a carry-over from Baroque.

---

[*] Rossini also wrote a Stabat Mater. See Appendix B.

From Bach to the Beatles – How Music Started

Near the middle 1800s, Opera changed to more emphasis on – for lack of a better term – power.

Sopranos and Tenors were featured (the high women's and men's voices) and the newer Opera composing led by Giuseppe Verdi (b. 1813) demanded full voice in the high range.

Still today, Soprano Divas and Tenors are the main Opera stars. And, yes, power is essential.

Opera can be divided into serious and comic. There's more about Comic Opera coming up in about six pages.

For serious Opera in the late 1800s, the drama intensified.

Verdi

Verdi's *Aida*, the story of a slave girl in Ancient Egypt is Grand Opera at its height (1871).

Settings of Pharaohs and pyramids add to the glory.

It is a tragedy: Aida dies at the end.

Performed usually without cats (see Chapter 3), <u>elephants</u> (L-ee-fahn-tz) have been used in the show.[*]

---

[*] Aida is pronounced "I-eee-duh". Verdi also wrote a Stabat Mater (Appendix B). It is a bald-faced lie that Verdi created the part of a Medieval Monk (munk) to tempt Aida to drink. That was never considered – ever. And that's the truth.

Elephant in *Aida*

Continuing in Italy

After Verdi, Italian Opera continued to grow behind the efforts of Pietro Mascagni, Ruggero Leoncavallo and maybe the greatest of all, Giacomo Puccini.

These guys had the good grace to NOT die until the 20th Century.

Mascagni wrote a dozen Operas with *Cavalleria Rusticana* the masterwork (1890) and Leoncavallo "hit" with *Pagliacci* (1892).

Puccini had a decade of success from 1893-1904 with *Manon Lescaut*, *La bohème*, *Tosca* and *Madama Butterfly*.

Wagner

A different kind of grandiose Opera is Richard Wagner's set of German works.

Wagner, born the same year as Verdi (1813), demands large orchestras.

(A lot of Wagner is loud! The brass section has much to do, and he makes good use of drums - some undoubtedly from Africa).

His melodies are sometimes continuous or "endless".

To explain: in *Tristan und Isolde* the *Liebestod* starts as a four-note theme overlaying a five-note strand. That's it – just nine notes! The beauty of the piece is how Wagner develops the simple theme.

He varies and builds the Music until the "tension" finally "releases" in a satisfying climactic moment.[*]

Wagner's masterwork is *Der Ring des Nibelungen* ("The Ring of the Nibelung"). It is a cycle of four complete Operas.

"Rick" Wagner took about 26 years to finish the *Ring*.

When all four Operas are performed together it lasts about 15 hours! So, each is generally done separately.

---

[*]For more on "tension and release", see Appendix H.

To learn how to pronounce Wagner's name, see the footnote near the beginning of Chapter 18 or simply look here: "Ree-kard Vawg-nerr".

From Bach to the Beatles – How Music Started

If I hear you correctly (and I usually do), you're saying: "Gee, that's a lot of Nibelung." Well, yes.

I suggest you introduce yourself to it in bits and pieces. But DO try some.

I'm not a staunch Wagner fan or heavy into Opera, but I strongly recommend listening to *Liebestod* (start and finish of *Tristan und Isolde*) and maybe the *Ride of the Valkyries*.

Put them on your "bucket" list (things to do before you "kick the" …uh… "glide off to the Happy Hunting Grounds").

I believe you will develop a more spiritually satisfied soul, free to pursue a life of intellectual fulfillment and endless passionate wanton lustful sensual desires of …

Uh … let's get back to matters at hand, so to speak.

Wagner and these four Italian masters were indisputable heavyweight members of the 1800s Opera scene.

To delve more into their individual contributions would not pay.

This book would probably weigh more than *War and Peace*.

(In Russian: "War-ski and Peace-nik".)*

---

* Isn't it just too cool? How I manage to mention *War and Peace* in conjunction with the next section - Russian Opera composers? Well, well.

From Bach to the Beatles – How Music Started

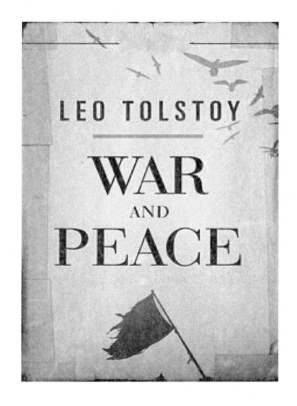

(A very BIG HEAVY Book)

Opera – Not-so-Funny

The following composers were also part of the Opera explosion which happened in the Nineteenth Century.

There were at least a half-dozen (7) Russian Opera composers, all of whom are fairly famous:

- Mikhael Glinka (d. 1857),
- Modest Mussorgsky (d. 1881),
- Alexander Borodin (d. 1887),
- Tchaikovsky (see Chapter 17 and Appendix E and H, d. 1893),
- Rimsky-Korsakov (see Chapter 17, d. 1908),
- Sergei Rachmaninoff (d. 1943), and
- Sergei Prokofiev (mentioned in Appendix C, d. 1953).

There's more about these guys – and a lot about Opera and Operetta in Book II.

Buy one.

You could also buy a copy of *War and Peace* ("War-ski and Peace-nik ") – if you want some "heavy" reading.

(Groan.)

Opera – Other Twigs

France

Since the middle ages, France had troubadours (see Glossary) and minstrels performing for the "everyman".

Then Paris blossomed with Opéra Comique, a form which was light Opera but not always funny. (Bizet's *Carmen* is tragic.)

All-but-forgotten names expanded Songs into light Opera stories throughout the 1700s.

Opera, when it did contain humor, was often frowned upon as "lower" or vulgar. Sometimes it was called vaudeville.

France, part deux

Around 1789, things got a little slicy / dicey in France.

That's when the revolting peasants gathered up King Louis and Marie Antoinette and prepared to separate their heads from the rest of their bodies.

Musicians had to be very careful what they wrote, for fear of being labeled an "enemy of the State" – or you, too, could find your head rolling in a basket.

From Bach to the Beatles – How Music Started

But the genre continued. Berlioz's _Damnation of Faust_ before 1850, Bizet's _Carmen_ (1875) and several works by Jacques Offenbach (b. 1819) found popularity through the 1800s.

Debussy, Paul Dukas and Ravel would carry on into the 20th Century.

<u>Opera - The Humerus Bone</u>

Comic elements in Opera are common. I already said that.

We just talked about the French Opéra Comique, full of farce (and often rife with lechery, bawdiness and innuendo).

Often there is a fine distinction among Opera with comic elements, Comic Opera and Operetta (or Musical Theater).

Operettas have lighter subject matter, some spoken parts and are designed more for the "common folk".

Humor in Opera took the following turn:

- Back in the day, Mozart and others had farcical situations in their Libretti (Classical and early Romantic Eras).
- Johann Strauss, Jr. (yes, the Waltz King) wrote more than a dozen Operettas – already mentioned at the end of Chapter 17, and they contain a lot of Comedy.
- Franz Lehar, also in Austria wrote Operettas into the 1930s. Most famous is his _Merry Widow_.
- England chimed in with perhaps the best-known Operettists ever – William S. Gilbert and Arthur Sullivan.

Gilbert and Sullivan collaborated on 15 Operettas from the 1870s to the 1890s.

By far, the most popular G & S Operettas are _H.M.S. Pinafore_, _Pirates of Penzance_ and _the Mikado_.

The fact that English was becoming the International Language definitely helped their popularity.

G & S Operettas poke unmerciful fun at "the Establishment", from Royal Navy to Government (yes, even Japanese).

In _Gondoliers_ (Venice, Italy) two idiots "share" power. It's very funny.

From Bach to the Beatles – How Music Started

So much for Europe and early Operettas. Things were also "popping" in the United States:

- Victor Herbert (Irish-German) wrote more than 40 musical plays through 1924.

  A couple good ones are *Cyrano de Bergerac* and *Babes in Toyland*.

- Sigmund Romberg (Austro-Hungarian) is best known for Operettas written in the 1920s, including *Desert Song*, *New Moon* and (very famous) his *Student Prince*.

  Prince is about life in Heidelberg, Germany, where this author had the good fortune to live several years.

- Rudolf Friml (also Austro-Hungarian) had success in the U.S. in the early 1900s with *Vagabond King*, *Three Musketeers* and *Rose-Marie*.

  Who can forget the movie *Rose Marie* when Nelson Eddy and Jeanette MacDonald introduce the song: *Indian Love Call* to the cinematic world?

We're slopping over, now, to what the next book (Part II) will contain.

Please remember to badger your book supplier and buy a copy – or several.

If you can't badger, maybe you otter.

(That pun is so bad, it's good. Well, maybe not.)

20. COMING ATTRACTIONS!

(A final summation and look forward to Book II.)

You may have noticed we live in the 21st Century. Well, Book II gets us there. There's a lot of Music yet to explore, starting about 1900.

You can expect:

- ❖ Scott Joplin and Ragtime (1890s), some of the swingin'- est sounds before the Swing Era.
- ❖ Early Jazz and Blues legends like:
  - Jelly Roll Morton,
  - Eubie Blake,
  - W.C. Handy,
  - Louis Armstrong.

Dance into the Roaring 20s with:[*]

- ❖ the Fox Trot,
- ❖ the Waltz (a carry-over from earlier),
- ❖ the Tango (sexy and South American),
- ❖ the Charleston (zippy and all American).

---

[*] They were called the Roaring 20s largely because the U.S. enacted Prohibition, making Booze (even Beer!) illegal. Jazz clubs "popped up" throughout cities and towns where people could drink, dance and carouse illegally. The music was fast and frantic, like the lifestyle. It all had to crash and did (1929).

From Bach to the Beatles – How Music Started

Spring forward in Popular Song with:
- ❖ Tin Pan Alley,*
- ❖ George Gershwin,
- ❖ Irving Berlin,
- ❖ Hoagy Carmichael.

Enjoy the transition to the Big Bands of the 30s and 40s:
- ❖ Tommy Dorsey,
- ❖ Jimmy Dorsey,
- ❖ Bennie Goodman,
- ❖ Duke Ellington,
- ❖ Count Basie,
- ❖ Glenn Miller.

These guys helped guide the careers of singers like Mel Torme, Frank Sinatra, Ella Fitzgerald, Billie Holiday, Peggy Lee and Doris Day.

The Tin Pan Alley and Big Band Musicians were vital to the morale of U.S. soldiers in World War II (1941-45) through their radio shows and live performances.

---

* Tin Pan Alley was a 2-block area on New York's Lower East Side where dozens of composers gathered to write and sell their Songs. A combination of thin walls and lots of "tinny" pianos banging out tunes led to the name.

From Bach to the Beatles – How Music Started

Explore the excitement of Broadway.* Operettas became Musicals and these flourished through the 1950s.

Early composers were:
- Victor Herbert,
- Sigmund Romberg,
- Rudolf Friml,
- Irving Berlin,
- George M. Cohan.

Soon came:
- Jerome Kern and Oscar Hammerstein,
- Richard Rodgers and Lorenz Hart,
- Alan Jay Lerner and Frederick Lowe,
- Cole Porter,
- George Gershwin.†

I should mention here that Florenz Ziegfeld began lavish stage works in New York around 1907. He founded his own Theater in 1927. One of his first presentations was Kern's and Hammerstein's *Showboat*, new and sensational.

---

* Broadway refers also to London's West End – increasingly a treasure of fresh and exciting Musicals.

† Herbert, Romberg and Friml are mentioned at the end of Chapter 19. Berlin and Gershwin are mentioned with Tin Pan Alley, above.

From Bach to the Beatles – How Music Started

Throw yourself into the "new" Broadway scene of the 50s, 60s and 70s. High on this list are:

- ❖ Rodgers and Hammerstein (now working together, beginning with the Pulitzer Prize winning *Oklahoma* (1943),
- ❖ Lerner and Lowe (continuing),
- ❖ Betty Comden and Adolph Green,
- ❖ Leonard Bernstein,
- ❖ Stephen Sondheim.

We would be remiss in not mentioning:

- ❖ Marvin Hamlisch,
- ❖ John Kander and Fred Ebb,
- ❖ Stephen Schwartz,
- ❖ Claude-Michel Schönberg and Alain Boublil and
- ❖ Andrew Lloyd Webber.

There are of course others like Meredith Willson (*Music Man*), Frank Loesser (*Guys and Dolls*), and Jerry Herman (*Hello Dolly*, *Mame* and *La Cage aux Folles*.)

A special mention goes to the choreography (dance) of performer / director Bob Fosse.

I could talk for hours – just about Musicals … but I won't.

From Bach to the Beatles – How Music Started

Lurch onward with Popular Music in the 50s when you:
- ❖ Combine Rhythm and Blues,
- ❖ Emphasize a strong Drum beat,[*]
- ❖ "Amp up" the newly invented Electric Guitar,
- ❖ Be unconventional in Music, hair and clothing,
- ❖ Invent new dances.

We call it <u>Rock and Roll</u>.

Give credit to Alan Freed who coined the phrase.

And let's salute the "first" rock guys:
- ❖ Chuck Berry,
- ❖ Bill Haley and the Comets.

Kudos to the followers, most of whom we have forgotten but not the "biggies" who include:
- ❖ Frankie Avalon,
- ❖ Paul Anka,
- ❖ Buddy Holly
- ❖ Elvis Presley (the King),
- ❖ The Beach Boys.

---

[*] If you don't know by now where Drums came from, I ain't a-goin' ta tell ya!

From Bach to the Beatles – How Music Started

Prepare to be invaded from Britain by:
- ❖ Herman's Hermits,
- ❖ The Rolling Stones,
- ❖ The Beatles – who culminated early Rock and Roll efforts and then led the way to "advanced" forms of Rock, starting later in the 1960s.

Experience the impact exerted on our culture by Country, Folk, Hillbilly, Bluegrass and Mountain Music.

* * *

As I so astutely mentioned in the first Chapter, Music did NOT die with the Beatles' breakup in 1971.

Our favorite kinds of Music live on. They continue to evolve.

If you enjoy Music - even one small percentage as much as I do …

If this whirlwind ride through Music Appreciation has helped get you to that point …

… well, it's been worth it.

Thanks for the journey.

* * *

(p.s. Remember to buy Book II. Maybe you'll get a discount. Not.)

From Bach to the Beatles – How Music Started

(This page is probably blank.)

(This one, too.)

Appendix A
BACH's Influence

WARNING !!!
THIS APPENDIX MAY BRING ON BOREDOM.
IT COULD INDUCE ENNUI IN GREAT QUANTITY!

Music was pretty DIS-organized up until Bach's time. His influence on organization and tonality was huge!

Bach invented or perfected many Musical Forms - notably the Fugue (Few-g), Chorale (Singing Choir), Cantata, and Concerto Grosso (Kon-chair-toe Yuck-o).

He put together a tuning method that modified the tonal distortion which happens as you "move away from" the "standard" scales of C, F and G. (You "adjust" the perfect intervals.)

With a "tempered" keyboard a composer could write and play Music in very disparate keys, sonically far removed from the closely-related scales. (Have I lost you yet?)

Bach did NOT discover this physical "gap" involving the overtone series. It's called the Pythagorean Comma (after the Ancient Greek, Aristotle Onassis), not the Bach-ian Comma.

He (Bach) used that knowledge to make Music and the Klavier (read Piano) easier to conceive and use. He (Onassis) used that knowledge to build ships and marry into the Kennedy clan.

From Bach to the Beatles – How Music Started

Appendix B
The Mass, Requiem and Stabat Mater

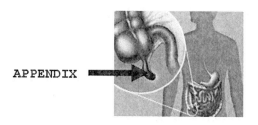

Remember the Holy Roman Empire? The Church-in-complete-charge? The Gregorian Chants? Well, <u>Masses</u> kind of started back then, stretching chants into full-blown religious "Musical Stories" praising God. The usual sections of the <u>Mass</u> were:

<u>Kyrie</u>   -   <u>Gloria</u>   -   <u>Benedictus</u>

<u>Agnus Dei</u>   -   <u>Amen</u>   and   <u>Good Riddance</u>

The <u>Requiem</u> (<u>Mass</u> for the Dead) is sort of like this (see Appendix C) - only you hafta first somehow get yourself deceased. The sections have different (weird) names, like Ralph and Martha.

A <u>Stabat Mater</u> does NOT translate to "Stab Your Mother." It has something to do with the sorrows of Jesus' Mother Mary.

Hey, what am I ... the medieval Church? Go ask a Monk (munk).

Appendix C
Some Other Important Musical Forms

Suite (Sweet) - a collection of Songs, Dances and Airs (heirs) for Instruments, loosely grouped, often for some special occasion (e.g. Handel's *Water Music*, played on a barge in the River Thames (Temms) for King George, who had his OWN boat).

Mass - Religious work for Voices and Instruments (see Appendix B).

Opera - Musical Story, with staging, mostly historical and/or mythical subjects, for Voices and Instruments - to be acted out.

Oratorio (Oreo) - an Opera without the staging, usually religious, simply sung, not acted (good with milk). Handel's *The Messiah* is the most famous one.

Concerto (Kon-chair-toe) - Piece for solo Instrument and Orchestra.

Concerto Grosso (Kon-chair-toe Yuck-o) - Piece for small group of "solo" Instruments with Orchestra (mainly Baroque Era.)

Chorale – Fairly simple religious Hymn, usually four-part, Soprano melody, vertical in style. Bach wrote tons of them. Even Martin Luther, the German priest wrote a famous one: *Ein' feste Burg ist unser Gott* ("A Might Fortress is our God").

From Bach to the Beatles – How Music Started

Appendix C (continued)
Some Other Important Musical Forms (continued)

Lieder (Lee-derr) - Just actual Songs, but a special name for those who speak German. They've been around since the Middle Ages and in other languages, too.

Schubert and Schumann kind of led the way…

Requiem (Wreck-we-am) - Church Service or Mass (mess) for the Dead. The basics were there back in Medieval (Gregorian) times but the Form really got going with Mozart, Berlioz and Brahms.

A Requiem is like a Mass with different section names (see Appendix B).

String Quartet - Chamber Music for four Stringed Instruments: 2 Violins, a Viola and a Cello (Chell-low).

Stabat Mater (See Appendix B).

Motet - The motet apparently arose from *clausula* sections, usually *strophic* interludes, in a longer sequence of *organum*, to which voices were added. Say, what? Actually, it just means musical notes with words sung to them. Duh.

Madrigal - A secular Song (meaning everyday, NOT religious). Sung usually by two to eight voices, Madrigals were the most important non-religious Songs of the Middle Ages. They are sometimes fun to sing today – just for variety.

Appendix C (continued)
Some Other Important Musical Forms (continued)

<u>Symphony</u> - Entire Orchestra in 3 or 4 or 5 Movements (For five Movements, see Beethoven and Berlioz).

As practiced by the Era's Big 3 Composers[*] the Classical Symphony developed into a fairly strict outline for four movements in closely-related keys:

(1) Sonata Allegro[†]   (2) "slow"
(3) Minuet (or Scherzo)[‡] (4) Finale.

> <u>V.I.I.N.</u> (<u>V</u>ery <u>I</u>mportant and <u>I</u>nformative <u>N</u>ote):
The Classical Symphony mentioned above is a Musical Form and is not to be confused with Sergei Prokofiev's <u>Classical Symphony</u>, No. 1 in D Major (Op 25), completed September 10, 1917, when my mother was seven months old.

<u>Ballet</u> (Pretty Dancers) – Story told with Orchestra and Dance. Most successful are French and Russian traditions, as well as "modern" American.

---

[*] We refer to the Big 3 in chapters 11, 13, Appendix D and the Index at the back of the book.

[†] For a really good look at Sonata Allegro Form, go to Appendix J. It's absolutely thrilling!

[‡] Scherzo is pronounced Scherzo

From Bach to the Beatles – How Music Started

Appendix D
Musical Eras

As long as people have been on "this here" planet there has been SOME kind of music. (See the first six Chapters of this book. Or you might want to investigate an actual <u>Music History Text</u>. How boring!)

"Experts" say Music wasn't well organized because PEOPLE weren't either (organized). This held true pretty much through the Roman Empire.

Then came the Dark Ages and, well… that was that for about a thousand years (roughly 450-1450). See Medieval. (I just ADORE saying that word!)

The Renaissance (Chapter 7) went well, at least for the Medicis. (Approximately 1450-1600.) It was a new start.

(Gee! So THAT's what the Renaissance means!)

The Baroque Period went from 1600 to 1750 and Classical started soon after that (until 1825), followed by Romantic and "Modern" (around 1900).

We don't have to debate – just point out a couple facts: J.S. Bach died in 1750, Handel in 1759. They stopped writing. Baroque pretty much stopped then.

A "transition" (<u>Rococo</u>) to Classical covers these times (roughly 1750-1770).

Appendix D (continued)
Musical Eras (continued)

Haydn (Hide-n), Mozart and Beethoven (the Classical "Big 3") were born in 1732, 1756 and 1770.

These three started writing when they were …oh… maybe 18 or 6 or 16.

Factor in poor sanitation, add the curvature of the Earth, divide by the Square Root of 37…

(Forget it!)

Appendix E
MOZART's Influence

100 years after Mozart lived, Ludwig von Köchel, another Austrian, catalogued Mozart's music. There are over 600 "K" numbers.

Mozart's Music is sensational. His Piano works (especially Concertos) are unequaled.

Of his Operas, two of the final three are very famous:

Cosi Fan Tutte (literally "Warm up your Derrière"), and

Die Zauberflöte ("Die, Sober Floater!") - a contemporary comment about drinking while swimming.

From Bach to the Beatles – How Music Started

Appendix E (continued)
MOZART's Influence (continued)

With Mozart Symphonies you can fly from lilting Melody to power rivaling Beethoven and Tchaikovsky. Numbers 40 (K550) and 41 (K551) are two of the best.

The dozen-or-more Instrumental Concertos include one not to be missed: The Clarinet Concerto in A Major, K622, written the year he died …uh… (sorry) … passed on.

In fact, fully 34 works were either written or completed in 1791, clearly his finest (though final) year.

I mention all this because Mozart's Music (along with the two Bachs' and Beethoven's) had such a powerful influence on future composers. Everybody says so. I'm just along for the ride.

Appendix F
Humor in Music

Humor - the Early Days

I'm sure some of the early writers had Senses of Humor. (They wrote in other languages back then, but hey! You never know!)

Let's see now … There's the Greeks and their thigh-slapping Choruses. Well, no.

Appendix F (continued)
Humor in Music (continued)

Humor - the Early Days (continued)

The Roman Matinees at the Colosseum involving
Christians and Lions and Bears ... Oh, my!
Lions and Christians and Bears ... Oh, my!
Follow the Yellow Brick Road.
Follow the Yellow Brick Road.*

But I digress ...

Ah ... the Medieval Monks (munks), busy decanting Wine and brewing Beer. Don't you suppose there was at least ONCE when the Abbott was away, they maybe launched into a chorus of _Ninety-nine Bottles of Beer on the Wall_?

The Holy Roman Empire had its hilarious moments. Like when the soldiers were marching those 18,256 hectares (Heck-tars) to Jerusalem on the Crusades. As they crossed the Alps can't you just hear them belting out a verse or two of _She'll be Coming 'Round the Mountain_.†

Did I mention those jocular Babylonians enjoying their Fuchsias (Few-shahs)? What a hoot.

---

* From that infamous gambling Movie: _The Wizard of Odds_.

† One hectare equals 631 wandoodles.

Appendix F (continued)
Humor in Music (continued)

Humor - the Early Days (continued)

And you can't beat Vivaldi's *4 Seasonings* for spicy variety! (That may be worth your "salt" - - - more humor!)

There's an unsupported historical rumor that Handel, in his final years, was working on one last Opera to be called *The 13 Funniest Months of the Year*. (The part of Month number 13 was to have been played by Jasper.)

This colossal work would have been performed on the River Thames (Temms) - no boats, just on the water! It would have included appropriate climate changes, swim vests, Federal Holidays, ski ropes, Red Cross volunteer lifeguards ...[*]

Humor - from Haydn

"Papa" Haydn's (Hide-enz) Music is filled with humor. Really.

He uses clever Instrument combinations and Rhythms to produce comical moments IN THE MUSIC.

---

[*] By "unsupported historical rumor", I mean I made it up.

Appendix F (continued)
Humor in Music (continued)

Humor - from Haydn (continued)

A favorite Haydn story is the "Farewell" Symphony (#45) when the musicians put out their lights and walk off the stage one-by-one during the final Movement, reportedly in protest of their treatment by the Prince.

(This kind of walk-out protest is NOT recommended in some of today's occupations, like …oh… Bus Drivers or Airline Pilots).

Some of Franz's Symphonies were called: the Bear, the Hen, the Fire, the Queen (oh?), the Echo – Echo – Echo - Echo.

The Surprise Symphony (#94) is famous because, in the quiet of the 2nd Movement, the Orchestra "blasts" out a "surprise" VERY LOUD CHORD - including Tympani.

(Yes, Tympani are Drums - from Africa).

There was even a set of early Symphonies neatly named *le matin*, *le midi* and *le soir* ("I Came, I Saw, I Hammer"). It may not be the *Four Seasons*, but …

Appendix F (continued)
Humor in Music (continued)

Humor - from Haydn (continued)

Some nicknames for Haydn String Quartets are: the Joke (plain enough), the Bird, the Frog, the Dream, the Lark, the Donkey and the Razor (NOT in a "sharp" key, rather F minor).

There's even one I call the Cha-Cha because that's what the final Movement sounds like.

Appendix G
BEETHOVEN's Influence

Beethoven's Music shows inventiveness at every turn. From bombastic (5th Symphony) to hauntingly beautiful ("Moonlight" Sonata), there is tremendous variety.

Ludwig's humor is not so much rib-tickling as it is subtle. Just look to the Symphonies for examples.

Beethoven's very first Symphony (#1) begins with a Dominant 7th chord. Very unusual and original.

Movement two is a clever Minuet (which normally occur in 3rd Movements).

Appendix G (continued)
BEETHOVEN's Influence (continued)

So Beethoven makes Movement three into a way-too-fast dance in three-quarter time, a Scherzo or "joke" (his invention).

Movement 4's intro gradually climbs a Major scale, again with a 7th (Dominant) added.

In the VERY somber Funeral March (Second Movement of Symphony #3) a Fugue (Few-g) tries to happen.

The 5th Symphony Finale Coda (tail end) includes 29 consecutive bars of C-chord. The Coda in #8 is even longer.

In the Beethoven seventh Symphony, Movement 2 has a single note Melody repeated for several measures.

Symphony #6 has five Movements, presaging Berlioz's *Symphonie Fantastique*. The "moods" depict the countryside, a brook, shepherds and other folk and a thunderstorm.

This sounds much like Rossini's *William Tell Overture* written 21 years later.

Beethoven never heard that *Overture*, because he was totally deaf and, besides, he had …uh… "shuffled off this mortal coil".

Appendix H
Emotion in Music

Let's start with Movie Music.

If you've ever felt a tear come to your eye at a sad movie moment . . .

If Director Alfred Hitchcock makes you jump out of your seat at a shower stabbing scene . . .

If horses racing across a western desert give you a thrill . . .

When the hero triumphs in the end . . .

Check out the Music!

Try watching the last five minutes of the Movie: _E.T. the Extraterrestrial_ and I'll bet you feel at least 3 different emotions.

You have to have a good story. But director Stephen Spielberg and composer John Williams collaborated excellently to create the perfect musical effects for the end of _E.T._

Spielberg then shot and edited that portion of the film to fit the emotion of the Music.

We respond physically to emotions. Music can play a big part eliciting or enhancing our feelings.

Appendix H (continued)
Emotion in Music (continued)

<u>Tricks that composers use:</u>

<u>Instrumental tricks</u> – Violins and Pianos are very effective for making us feel sad. I am a sucker for a French Horn.

For happiness, a thrill, excitement - bring out the brass (Trumpets, Trombones) and Tympani and Snare Drums (and …yes… they probably do come from Africa).

Make it loud.

<u>Construction tricks</u> – The biggie here is "tension and release". Writers build tension by beginning low (in pitch), slow speed, soft (volume).

(The notes used can be "dissonant". They can grate on our ears).

We want this tension to go away, to be resolved, to make us more comfortable.

So, you as the composer bring these elements toward their opposites (i.e. louder, higher, faster and into consonance - pleasing to our ears) and thereby release the tension.

Appendix H (continued)
Emotion in Music (continued)

A few examples:

- *E.T.* – the ending of the movie (already mentioned).

- Bach's *Toccata and Fugue in D minor* (the famous one), the fugue Development and ending.*

- Randall Thompson's *Alleluia*, the build up and climactic loud part near the end.

- Almost any section of Tchaikovsky's 5th Symphony.

- The "shower" scene from the Movie: *Psycho*. Listen through to the very end of the scene and hear how Bernard Herrmann's perfect musical score sets the tension and releases it.

Silent Movies.

From 1900 to 1930 or so, there were Movies without sound. Most theaters hired Organists to accompany the show with appropriate Music.

---

* For more about The Fugue (Few-g) and Development, I refer you to Chapter 8, Appendix J and possibly Appendix A.

Appendix H (continued)
Emotion in Music (continued)

Special Theater Organs had all kinds of attachments – bells, drums, pipes, Auto horns… The Organist could make just about any sound to add to the screen action. And highlight emotion.

Wait a minute … back to "classical" Music.

Gregorian Chants are somber. Medieval (love that word!) Songs and Dances are lively. But musical emotions really developed through the Classical Era and into the Romantic Era.

Bigger Orchestras, better Instruments and having the Music "fit" a scene – these were factors leading to more emotion in the Music.

- Berlioz' wild "Witches Dance" in the *Symphonie Fantastique*,
- Dvorak's New World melodies (Symphony #9),
- Debussy's programme pieces about the Moon, the Sea and a Faun (like a Satyr, half human, half goat) and
- Grieg's *Peer Gynt*

 are just four examples showing great emotion.

 Opera unabashedly "oozes" emotion![*]

---

[*] See Chapters 16 through 19 for more about the Romantic Era, including Opera.

Appendix I
UNDER THE Influence

(Hic!)

Appendix J
Counterpoint and Development

Now remember ... Did you wear your hip boots like I said? I warned you.

Here goes - we'll try to go at a moderate pace, so you non-musicians will not get lost, nor will you actual musicians get too bored too soon.

Counterpoint

From the Latin: *punctus contra punctus* (meaning: "Monk (munk), Bring me more Beer, Monk (munk)!")

Counterpoint (n.); Counter-Melody (n.); Contrapuntal (adj.); meaning against or counter to the main Melody (wgas.)

Reminder: a Melody is simply a tune.

A basic example is *Row, Row, Row Your Boat*. Sung by one person, it's an easy kids' song.

When we sing it as a "Round", a second voice starts a little later with 3rd and 4th voices after that.

Gently Down the Stream forms a harmonic (easy on the ear) second Melody which goes well with the first tune.

From Bach to the Beatles – How Music Started

Appendix J (continued)
Counterpoint and Development (continued)

The *Merrily, Merrily, Merrily, Merrily* part is even better Counterpoint when sung (or played) "against" the other Melodies, because it has rhythmic variation.

And *Life is but a Dream*, the fourth part, provides a solid ending. Put it all together and it rings nicely.

So you see a "Round" (Row-un-d) is simple Counterpoint. Sometimes it's called Canon (Boom).

Counterpoint generally follows the prevailing Harmony (that means it is "in tune"). Rather than "vertical" chords, the result is a "horizontal" harmonic flow.

Band composer John Phillip Sousa wrote mostly Marches. He uses Counter-Melodies very effectively at the end of his March Trios.

(The Trio is the "middle" part, different from the first part.)

In the *Stars and Stripes Forever*, the Trio is played once "straight". Second time through, he adds the famous Piccolo descant (a high-pitched Counter-Melody).

Finally, a strong Trombone Counterpoint is added.

Appendix J (continued)
Counterpoint and Development (continued)

The most complex contrapuntal style is probably the Fugue (Few-g). Four voices enter canonically, one-by-one, usually a 5th apart, lowest voice last.

The resulting transitions, segues (say-gg-ways) and general horizontal mixings can be terrific.

I marvel at how composers do that. I could not pull it off.

Take a look on the next page at the refrain - *Gloria* - from *Angels We Have Heard on High*, a Christmas Song. As usual, Sopranos (the top line) sing the melody.

(If you do not read Music, I explain that there are 4 VOICES represented here. From top to bottom, they are Soprano, Alto, Tenor and Bass. In this example, the bottom three VOICES are contrapuntal.)

Notice the harmonic Counterpoint in the Alto, Tenor and Bass (which also happens to be a good example of Fifth Fall),[*] each very different and adding uniquely to the overall harmonic effect. I think we've all heard this Song – at least I hope so.

---

[*] How a Fifth Fall progression works is interesting, but will have to wait until another day for discussion.

Appendix J (continued)
Counterpoint and Development (continued)

Gloria (refrain) from *Angels We Have Heard on High*.

Appendix J (continued)
Counterpoint and Development (continued)

<u>Development</u> – the last item, I promise!

Renaissance and Baroque writers started developing (expanding) musical themes. The idea came to near-perfection in the Classical Era.

Sonata-Allegro form.

Sonata form states a theme (A) and an answer (B), usually repeats it, contrasts it with another theme and answer (C) and (D), repeated. This is called the <u>Exposition</u>.

<u>Development</u> is the central portion of this form. Composers chop, stretch and shrink (*fragment, augment and diminute*) the themes and range all over Left Field with key changes. It can be quite a ride!

The real Art is to corral the well-developed threads so as to re-state them in original form and key. This is the <u>Recapitulation</u>.

Sonata form ends here. There can be an added <u>Coda</u>[*] - a short extension (unless you're Beethoven, who often exceeds SHORT by several minutes).

---

[*] See Chapter 13 and Appendix G, Beethoven and Codas.

(This page is SUPPOSED to be a blank)

INDEX of Composers

Composer	**Chapter**
3 B's Greatest composers (see also Big 3 Classical composers)	17 (It's confusing)
5, "Russian", the (Stasov, Balakirev, Cui, Rimsky-Korsakov, Borodin and Mussorgsky. I know there are six. What do you want ME to do about it?)	17
Arne	19
Bach, C.P.E.	11, 13, Appendix E
Bach, J.S.	1, 6, 8, 9, 12, 13, Appendix A, Appendix D, Appendix E, Appendix H
Bach, P.D.Q.	14 (footnote)
Beatles, The	1, 13, 20, Book II
Beethoven	6, 11, 13, 14, 16, 19, Appendix C, Appendix D, Appendix E, Appendix G, Appendix J, Goldilocks and the Three Bears
Bellini	19
Berg	13, 18, Book II
Berlioz (see also Plot to Kill, *Symphonie Fantastique*, *Dies Irae* and weird in the Glossary.)	13, 16, 19, Appendix C, Appendix G, Appendix H

INDEX of Composers

Composer	Chapter
Bernstein (see Dvorak and Mahler)	18, 20, Book II
Berry, Chuck	13, 20, Book II

𝕭𝕴𝕲 3

Big 3 Classical composers (see also the 3 B's Greatest composers)	11, 13, Appendix D, (It's too confusing)
Bizet	19
Blow	19
Boccherini	10, 14
Borodin	19
Botticelli (artist)	7
Brahms	13, 16, 17
Buxtehude (see Scandinavia)	9, Glossary
Byrd	7, 13
Chopin	16
Clementi	14

INDEX of Composers

Composer	**Chapter**
Corelli	10, 14
Couperin (see also Ravel)	10, 18
Debussy	18, Appendix H
Donizetti	19
Dvorak	18, 19, Appendix H, Book II
Eberl	13 (footnote)
Friml	19, 20
Gabrieli	7
Gilbert (see also Sullivan)	19
Glinka	19
Gluck	11, 19
Grieg	18, Appendix H
Handel	9, 19, Appendix C, Appendix D, Appendix F
Haydn (Hide-n)	6, 11, 12, Appendix D, Appendix F
Herbert	19, 20
Herrmann (*Psycho*)	Appendix H, Book II
Lassus	7

INDEX of Composers

Composer	Chapter
Lehar	19
Leoncavallo	19
Lizq#s?t (and his relatives Christmas, Shopping and Laundry)	16
Lully	19
Mahler	18, 19
Mascagni	19
Mendelssohn	16
Mozart	6, 9, 11, 14, 19, Appendix D, Appendix E
Mussorgsky (see Ravel.)	18, 19
Offenbach	19
Pachelbel (Tah-co-bell)	9, 13 (footnote)
Paganini	16
Palestrina	7
Pergolesi	10, 14
Peri – first Opera (lost)	19
Praetorius	7
Prokofiev	17, 19, Appendix C, Book II

INDEX of Composers

Composer	Chapter
Puccini	19, Book II
Purcell	9, 19
Rachmaninoff (see Paganini)	16, 19
Rameau	10, 19
Ravel (see also: *Bolero* in the Glossary.)	18, 19
Rimsky-Korsakov	17, 19, Book II
Romberg	19, 20
Rossini	16, 19, Appendix G
Scarlattis, the	9, 11, 19
Schoenberg	18, Book II
Schubert (not to be confused with Schumann)	14, 16
Schumann (not to be confused with Schubert)	16, 17
Schultze (see Praetorius)	
Schütz	19
Sousa (March King) (see Counterpoint in The Glossary.)	Appendix J, Book II
Strauss, Johann, II (Joe, Jr.)	17, 19

INDEX of Composers

Composer	**Chapter**
Strauss, Richard ("Ree-card", no relation to Joe Jr.)	17, Book II
Stravinsky	17, 18, Book II
Sullivan (see also Gilbert)	19
Tchaikovsky	17, 19, Appendix E, Appendix H
Telemann	11
Thompson (*Alleluia*)	Appendix H
Verdi	19, Book II
Vivaldi	9, 19, Appendix F
Von Weber	19
Wagner (see also Strauss or Debussy)	17, 18 (name pronunciation), 19
Webber, Andrew Lloyd (I list all his names here because (1) he is still alive and (2) he is famous and filthy rich.)	16, Book II
Webern	18
Zelda (honorary token person for all the females who wrote Music but were never discovered and therefore we don't know them.)	

KEEP GOING! ⟶

(This Blank is SUPPOSED to be a page!)

GLOSSARY

Reference

Chapter

Reference	Chapter
3 B's Greatest composers (see also Big 3 Classical composers)	17 (It's confusing)
5, "Russian", the (Stasov, Balakirev, Cui, Rimsky-Korsakov, Borodin and Mussorgsky. (See Index)	17
America	8, 13 (footnote), 14, 17, 18, 19, 20
Aristotle (see also Pythagorus)	Appendix A
Australia	19
Austria	12, 13, 14, 17, 18, 19
Babylon	3, 19, Appendix F
Babysitting (and / or changing diapers)	Nowhere in THIS book!
Baloney (Bologna, in Italy)	19 (footnote)
Baroque	8, 9, 10, 11
Barry, Dave	Mentioned in Chapter 19 as a tribute.
Beach, Sunova	Forewarning
Beer (not to be confused with Bier)	Author, Author! 4, Fore! 5
Bier (not to be confused with Beer)	A funeral pyre, but also the German word for Beer.

GLOSSARY

Reference   **Chapter**

Reference	Chapter
Big 3 Classical composers (see also the 3 B's Greatest composers)	11, 13, Appendix D, (It's too confusing)
Bills, Monthly (see also Checks, Bank)	Dedication Page
Bolero (see also Ravel, 1984 Olympic Ice Dancing, Torvill and Dean)	18, Book II
Borgia Family	7, 8 (footnote)
Botticelli (artist)	7
Cake, Black Forest Cherry (see also Haydn-in-the-Busch)	Author, Author!
Canon (Boom) (see Counterpoint)	Appendix J
"Caterpillar crossing the Road" riddle	Author, Author! (Find the answer somewhere in this book, in a chapter to-be-self-discovered-by-you yourself alone, with nobody. (It could be in a footnote!?!?)

GLOSSARY

Reference	**Chapter**
Cello (Chell-low) – about 5-times bigger than a Violin, held between the knees and spiked to the floor. This is why Cellists do not move around much.	Just thought you'd like to know.
Checks, Bank (see also Bills, Monthly)	Title Page
Classical Era	11, 12, 13, 14
Columbus (see also Colombo, Corombo, Cincinnati, Cleveland and Peoria)	16, Paganini
Concerto	Appendix C
Coolidge, Calvin (U.S. President, deceased)	9 (footnote)
Counterpoint (see also Development)	Appendix J
Czechoslovakia (once-upon-a-time country)	18
Da Vinci Code, the (see Movies)	
Dark Ages (see also Feminine Inequality)	4, Fore! 15, Appendix D
Dave Barry (see Barry, Dave)	
Death, hideous (see Opera)	19
Denmark (see Scandinavia)	This Glossary
De Rigueur Mortis (see Opera)	19
Development (see also Counterpoint)	Appendix J

GLOSSARY

Reference	Chapter
Die, Sober Floater! (*Die Zauberflöte*)	Appendix E
Dies Irae or Day of Wrath (see also Berlioz, Grapes, Monks)	16 (footnote)
Disclaimer	11
Disney World (see Early Opera)	19
Dissonance (as opposed to Consonance)	11 (Scarlatti), 18 (footnote), Appendix H
Drums	4, Fore! 5, 6, 9 (footnote), 12 (footnote), 13, 14 (footnote), 17 (footnote), 18, 20 (footnote), Appendix F, Appendix H, Book II
Earth, Curvature of the	Appendix D
Egypt	3, 8 (footnote), 9, 19 (Opera, Verdi)
Elephants (see Verdi, *Aida*)	19
Emotion in Music	15, Appendix H
England	9, 13, 14, 16, 17, 18, 19, 20
Eras, Musical	Appendix C, Appendix D
Europe, Central, Map of	12
Feminine Inequality (see also Dark Ages)	4, Fore! 15, Appendix D
Ferrari (see also Lamborghini)	10

GLOSSARY

Reference   Chapter

Reference	Chapter
Finland (see Scandinavia)	This Glossary
Florida (see Early Opera)	19
France	10, 14, 16, 18, 19
French Impressionist Painters (see a good reputable Art Museum)	Louvre, the
Fuchsias (Few-shahs)	3, 6, 8 (footnote), 19
Galileo (scientist)	7
Games, Olympic (see also *Bolero*)	10, 18
Germany	9, 13, 14, 16, 17, 18, 19
Granddaughter, my	8
Greece	3, 8 (footnote), 9, Appendix F
Gregorian (Gray-Gory-Ann) Chant	4, Fore! 5
Gutenberg (printer)	6
Harmony	2, 3, 4, Fore! 17
Haydn-in-the-Busch (see also Cake, Black Forest Cherry)	Author, Author!
"Hey, Dudes" (see Chopin in Index)	16
Holy Roman Empire	4, Fore! Appendix F

GLOSSARY

Reference	Chapter
Humor in Music	Appendix F, and hopefully dispersed liberally throughout this Book and Book II.
Hungary	12, 16, 18
Hypotenuse (Don't ask.)	3
Iraq	3, 8 (footnote), 9
Italy	7, 8 (footnote), 9, 10, 11, 14, 16, 18, 19
Killing and Raping	5, 7
Knobby and his Magic Banana	18, Mahler
Lamborghini (see also Ferrari)	10
Libretto - Story (See Opera)	19
Lieder (Lee-derr.) There's a hilarious joke involving the punch line: "take me to your Lieder, I'll see your Ladder Later". Or perhaps not.	14, 16, 17
Machiavelli (thinker)	7
Mass (see also Mess)	Appendix B, Appendix C
Medici Family	7, 8 (footnote)
Medieval - Middle Ages (Just practicing the spelling. It's such a cool word!)	5, 6, Appendix D, Appendix F

GLOSSARY

Reference	Chapter
Melody	2, 3, 4, Fore! 17
Mess (see also Mass)	Look anywhere in this book
Mesopotamia (a mythical land)	3, 9
Michelangelo (artist)	7
Middle Ages (see also Medieval)	5, 6, Appendix D, Appendix F
Minstrels (see also Troubadours)	5
Monks (munks) (see also Beer, Wine and Medieval – LOVE that word!)	4, Fore! 9 (footnote), 12 (footnote), 13 (footnote), 14 (footnote), 16 (footnote), 18, 19 (footnote), Appendices E, F, I, and J
Movie: *Court Jester* (with Danny Kaye)	18 (footnote), Book II
Movie: *Da Vinci Code, the*	13
Movie: *E.T.: The Extraterrestrial*	Appendix H, Book II
Movie: *Ghost*	3
Movie: *History of the World, Part I*	2
Movie: *Master and Commander: The Far Side of the World*	10, 14
Movie: *Psycho*	Appendix H, Book II
Movie: *Rose Marie*	19

GLOSSARY

Reference	**Chapter**
Movie: *Wizard of Odds, The*	Appendix F
Movies, Silent	Appendix H, Book II
Musical Forms	Appendix A, Appendix C, Appendix J
Nothing Important	Explains an awful lot of this so-called "expert" book.
Norway (see Scandinavia)	This Glossary
Og (and other Cavemen)	2
Opera	19, Appendix C, Appendix E, Appendix H
Opera Houses	19
Operetta	17, 19, 20, Book II
Paris – City of Lights. This author found a strange affinity in 1981, grew a beard and hasn't shaved since. It's in France, which also has a lot of French people. (See Couperin, Rameau, Berlioz, Debussy, Bizet, Ravel, Charles De Gaulle and Gene Kelly, among others.)	10, 16, 18, 19, Index
Pictures at an Exhibition (see Ravel)	18
Poland (see Chopin)	16

GLOSSARY

Reference	Chapter
Pythagorus (see also Aristotle)	Appendix A
Renaissance (or Renascimento)	7, Appendix D
Requiem	Appendix B, Appendix C, 13, (Mozart), 16 (Berlioz), 17 (Brahms), 18 (Dvorak)
Rhythm	2, 3, 4, Fore! 17
Rococo	11
Romantic	16, 17, 18, 19
Rome	4, Fore! 8 (footnote), 16, Appendix F
Round (see Counterpoint or Canon, boom!)	Appendix J
Russia	12, 17, 18, 19
Ruth, Babe	12, Baseball Hall of Fame
Scandinavia (Very cold - The part of the World where nobody comes from, at least not on purpose, until the Romantic Era. Consists of Denmark, Finland, Norway, Sweden and Lap Land for those who wish to sit. See Buxtehude or Grieg.)	9 or 18, This Glossary, Index
Shakespeare (writer)	16
Spain	11, 14

GLOSSARY

Reference	Chapter
Stabat Mater (see Scarlatti, Vivaldi, Haydn, Schubert, Dvorak, Verdi and Rossini)	9 (twice), 12, 14, 18, 19 (twice), (in that order), Appendix C
Strange First Names (see Berlioz or Rimsky-Korsakov's wife)	16, 17
Strange French Musical Names (see Debussy)	18
Strange Scales (see Debussy or Strange Fish)	18 (footnote)
String Quartet - 2 Violins, 1 Viola and 1 Cello (Chell-low.) See Haydn.	12, Appendix C
Suite (Sweet)	Appendix C
Sweden (see Scandinavia)	This Glossary
Sympathy (something you do NOT get from us for trying to read this book.)	
Symphonie Fantastique (see also Berlioz and weird)	16 (Berlioz), Appendix G, Appendix H
Symphony	Appendix C
Timbre (Tam-burr) - something Music has. It's the special tone quality of an instrument that sets it apart from others. Do NOT skip this footnote!	18 (footnote)

GLOSSARY

Reference   **Chapter**

Tome (Toh-m) - a popular first name in
    America such as Tome Sawyer
    (see Mark Twain in some other
    book), the actor / boat racer,
    Tome Crews and Tome S. Edison,
    famous inventor.   16 (footnote)

Troubadours (see also Minstrels)   5

Viennese School, Second   11, 18

Viola – slightly larger than a Violin,
    played similarly, held under
    the chin.   Thought you'd like to know.

War and Peace - A HUGE, HEAVY book
    written by some Russian guy.
    (Tall Story, I think his name was.) 19

Whip-Poor-Will (either a bird or a terrible
    thing to do to a sad kid named
    Billy-Boy.)   Not important - I just like saying
                                      the word.

Wife, Donna   11, 17, Dedication, Author, Author!

Wine   4, Fore!

Zarathustra   Don't know. Just threw it in here.
                                      Thought I'd end with a Z-word, so
                                      I can claim to have "thus spake"
                                      everything from America to
                                      "Zarathustra".

Please continue . . .

p.s. You can write your OWN notes here!

On this page, which would normally be blank – and admittedly for the purpose of self-preservation in the face of otherwise devastating attacks by hoards of jealous contributors – the author chooses to acknowledge the contributions of several individuals toward the successful completion of the book.

- ✓ To my wife, I'm amazed at her eternal love.
- ✓ To my car, I marvel at its internal combustion.
- ✓ To my mother, I praise her maternal ministrations.
- ✓ To my cat, I thrill to her fraternal compulsions.
- ✓ To my children, I exasperate at their infernal consumptions.

On a serious note:

- ✓ Kudos to <u>Casey McEneny</u> and <u>Jon Zagel</u> at Newport High School, Oregon for their support and coordination.
- ✓ A large and smiling nod of the noggin to <u>Rose Reed</u> at Newport Lazerquick Printers for all her work preparing and printing the manuscript.
- ✓ To all the folks at Aardvark Publishing. I couldn't have done it without you.
- ✓ To the many readers who pointed out my various follies, but whose counsel I chose mostly to ignore . . . Ha!
- ✓ (But serially, thanks).

There are two ways you can buy this book:
(1) Paperback by contacting the publisher at
    Aardvark Publishing
    P.O. Box 173
    Seal Rock OR 97376
        or
(2) On-line through Amazon.com.
    They will mail you a paperback copy
    or sell you the "Kindle" version.

    The money will go to good use. My grandchildren will thank you – as they dawdle in luxury along the Riviera.